DIFFICULT
IS THE
Path

*Why Life as a Disciple of Jesus Is
Not for the Fainthearted*

R. RODERICK CYR

CROSSBOOKS
PUBLISHING

CrossBooks™
A Division of LifeWay
1663 Liberty Drive
Bloomington, IN 47403
www.crossbooks.com
Phone: 1-866-879-0502

All Scripture is quoted from the New King James version unless otherwise noted. Copyright 1979, 1980, 1982 by Thomas Nelson, inc. Used by permission. All rights reserved. Scripture quotations marked NLT are taken from the Holy Bible, New Living Translation, copyright 1996, 2004. Used by permission of Tyndale House Publishers, Inc., Wheaton, IL 60189. All rights reserved. Scripture quotations marked NIV taken from the HOLY BIBLE, NEW INTERNATIONAL VERSION. Copyright 1973, 1978, 1984 Biblica. Used by permission of Zondervan. All rights reserved.

First published by CrossBooks 03/19/2013

ISBN: 978-1-4627-2623-3 (sc)
ISBN: 978-1-4627-2622-6 (hc)
ISBN: 978-1-4627-2624-0 (e)

Library of Congress Control Number: 2013904659

Printed in the United States of America

This book is printed on acid-free paper.

For the Lord,
who makes the difficult path worth pursuing.

TABLE OF CONTENTS

INTRODUCTION

T wo thousand years ago Jesus declared that following Him would not be easy. He informed potential followers, "narrow is the gate and difficult is the way which leads to life, and there are few who find it" (Matthew 7:14). The call of Christ represents a real challenge and requires significant discipline from anyone wanting to be His disciple. Believers face daily hurdles in living consistent with Jesus' commands because obedience does not come naturally due to our sin nature. Following Jesus exerts substantial cost in every area of life including:

- Relationships.
- Careers.
- Time.
- Money.
- Reputations.
- Friendships.
- Comfort.
- Dreams.
- Lifestyles.
- Priorities.

Although the path of discipleship proves difficult, God equips us to make the journey. He challenges us through His word, brings along other believers who encourage us and help us endure, and sends His

Holy Spirit to empower us in opposing sin. We encounter a difficult path as we pursue Jesus, but He sustains us.

Despite Jesus' teaching about the difficult path, in America we often learn that faith makes life more comfortable not more difficult. That perspective, however, has no basis in Scripture. The Bible never suggests submission to Jesus produces a more leisurely, pleasurable, or "successful" life. A life filled with joy? Yes. A more satisfying life? Sure. A life we find more rewarding? Absolutely. Indeed, we receive countless benefits upon coming to faith in Jesus, but having an easier, more comfortable life is not one of them. Although its genesis is unclear, this doctrine has exploded across denominational lines and taken root in conservative, liberal, and evangelical churches alike over the past several decades.

However, despite receiving an especially accommodating audience in our churches, this message contradicts Scripture and leads followers down a path that's both unfruitful and destructive. It produces an impotent and unproductive faith that thrives in our "me-centric" culture. It aligns with our selfish and worldly society and has led to an explosion of casual Christians who view faith through the lens of selfishness (how we benefit as believers) rather than through the lens of sacrifice (how we serve God and others). We want a faith that affirms our lifestyle as legitimate and a God who yearns to show His love by taking care of our needs, making us happy, and wants desperately to bless us. We want a God who makes no demands of us and requires little substantive change in our lives.

As a result, vast numbers of professing believers live a faith that barely resembles the life to which Jesus beckons us. So egregious is this doctrinal error that many of those who embrace it likely possess no real faith in Jesus at all. They have submitted to a faith that adheres to the desires of the flesh and has its foundation in the world. We must refute this dangerous doctrine before it further erodes the power and life of the American church. America needs more believers who fully embrace the call of Christ and live the difficult life of discipleship. We need more pastors boldly proclaiming these truths and conveying what a life following Jesus means. If we do not begin to live more fully the gospel Jesus gave us, this country will continue its rapid decline and never experience the revival it desperately needs. "Now it is high time to awake out of sleep, for now our salvation is nearer than when we first believed" (Romans 13:11b). We must become vigilant and wake each other up from our spiritual slumber. No more compromise with the culture. No more softening the truth because pastors fear their congregants will leave; even many of Jesus' followers left Him on learning His expectation for them and how difficult their lives would become. (See John 6:65-66).

This book examines Scripture to discover what Jesus taught regarding the lifestyle of anyone who calls Him Lord. We study Jesus' lessons and declarations to understand why following Him represents a difficult path. We explore the epistles to learn what the apostles say about the call of Christ and the challenge it presents. We review numerous passages that reinforce the message that an authentic faith does not come easily. Many readers will discover teachings and commands from Jesus with which they are unfamiliar. Others will find themselves greatly resisting the truths Jesus and His disciples proclaim. Avoid dismissing the lessons simply because they feel uncomfortable or are foreign. Instead, pray through the difficult messages. Seek guidance from the Lord and ask the Holy Spirit to reveal truth to you. Most of all, search the Scriptures diligently and confirm what the Bible says and what the Lord taught.

Additionally, readers may find value in studying this book in a small group and benefiting from a thorough discussion of each chapter with like-minded believers. Such a format also allows readers to hold each other accountable in applying what they learn, as well as encouraging each other as you embark down the "difficult path that leads to life." To facilitate discussion, several questions conclude each chapter. These questions challenge the reader to reflect on the substance of the relevant Scripture and identify specific actions he or she can take in response to God's truth. You can use these questions by yourself or with a study group.

I close with a couple comments about the style and focus of this book. Throughout the book I use the masculine pronoun "he" in discussing the individual believer. I do so for ease of readability but every instance refers to both male and female believers. I hope my readers will extend a little grace on this issue and not take offense.

While the Scripture we examine applies to believers everywhere, the book focuses on American believers and our response to the lessons Jesus taught. I believe most of us struggle with applying the scriptural truths we explore and therefore periodically direct comments and challenges to the American church and believer. I do this out of tremendous concern and love for the body of believers in the United States, and with the hope that doing so contributes to the revival God wants to bring to this country.

Readers will note I use few anecdotes in the book. I prefer referencing the parables and metaphors Jesus employed, which are much more effective in communicating His truth. Since much of what we discuss involves challenging principles, we often examine Scriptures that share a similar lesson or message. While this may appear redundant at times, it is by design. Jesus addresses these subjects on multiple occasions and His emphasis establishes their importance. Our failure to apply them in our lives magnifies the need to stress them through examination of multiple passages.

Many of the books sold in Christian bookstores today make the reader feel good about himself and his faith. Often they stroke our egos, diminish our sin, affirm our spirituality, and emphasize 'us' in our relationship with God. They often fail to challenge believers, make us uncomfortable, or raise difficult questions about the legitimacy of what we believe. This is not one of those books.

This book makes no effort to reinforce your centrality to the gospel, does not discuss the depths of God's love for you, and invests little time identifying the benefits you accrue on becoming a Christian. Innumerable books address those topics to the point that many of us believe such concepts characterize the essence of Christianity. This book takes a decidedly different path; a more difficult path, if you will. We investigate the thorny lessons Jesus taught and the challenging parables He communicated to His disciples. We discover how to apply them in our lives and why they are so difficult to implement. Many will find the discussions unsettling, but I encourage you to work through them and experience the spiritual growth that results.

Finally, let me add a note about how I came to write this book. The Lord burdened my heart for more than two decades with the Scriptures identified and discussed herein. During that time I struggled with several questions relating to each of these verses. How do I apply the verses in my life in a substantive way, more than mere acquiescence? How do I live these verses as Jesus wants me to live them? Why do so few pastors and Christian leaders teach these truths to their congregants? Why do so many ignore these verses or water them down to irrelevance when addressing them?

This book represents a challenge to the American church to understand and apply the difficult verses Jesus taught. In addition, it is a call to pastors and Christian leaders alike to begin preaching the sacrificial life a disciple of Jesus lives, the difficult path Jesus calls every follower of His to pursue. As such teaching becomes increasingly prevalent across the church in America and as Christians increasingly follow the path of discipleship Jesus calls us to take, I believe the Lord will bring the revival we urgently need in this country.

Maranatha,
Roderick

PART I

Difficult because: We Must Believe

What do you value more, what someone says they will do or what they actually do? For example, if a friend agrees to pick you up at the airport at 9pm but never shows, are you appreciative of his verbal commitment to help? Do you thank him for at least expressing a willingness to pick you up even though he never follows-through with his promise? Does it matter if he tells you he became distracted doing something he enjoyed or lost track of time hanging out with someone else? If you had agreed to give him $100 for picking you up, would you pay him the money if he never shows up? I doubt any of us would pay him the $100 because what matters is that the friend actually picks you up and not simply agrees to pick you up. Verbally agreeing to some action rarely has value if not followed up with the action agreed.

Similarly, if a friend tells you, "I love you" but never demonstrates love in action, then of what value are the words? If your friend never wants to spend time with you, does not enjoy talking with you, and ignores your request for help in time of need, you would rightfully assume that he or she does not really love you. Their love is in words only, which is not really love at all.

Whenever someone's actions are inconsistent with their words, we tend to agree that the actions reflect what they really believe. However frequently someone says something and no matter the passion with

1

which they make a claim, if their actions do not align then they probably do not really mean what they say.

The same holds true on matters of faith. If we passionately assert we believe in God, then our lives ought to reflect that. If we claim we love Jesus but rarely spend time with Him, show little interest in building a relationship with Him, and never respond to His calls, then how genuine is our claim? If we profess Jesus as Lord but only follow His will when convenient, obey only His commands with which we agree, and sacrifice only those areas of life we find easy, then it is doubtful He is really Lord.

Numerous passages in the Bible discuss this issue. They address the inconsistency between what people say about their relationship with God and how they live their faith. Scripture informs us that what matters is what we really believe, not just what we claim to believe. And what we really believe is evidenced by our lifestyle, behavior, decisions, priorities, and such.

In the first two chapters of this book we explore Scripture to understand the difference between saying you believe and actually believing. We discuss the impact each has on the life of the believer.

Not everyone who says to me, "Lord, Lord" shall enter the kingdom of heaven, but he who does the will of My Father in heaven. Many will say to Me in that day, "Lord, Lord, have we not prophesied in Your name, cast out demons in Your name, and done many wonders in Your name?" And then I will declare to them, "I never knew you, depart from Me, you who practice lawlessness."

—Matthew 7:21-23

CHAPTER 1

Insincere Faith

In an effort to simplify the gospel, American churches frequently ask unbelievers to pray the "Sinner's Prayer" as the requirement for becoming a Christian. Reciting the prayer makes you a believer and provides salvation. In addition, most churches teach new believers the doctrine, "Once saved, always saved," otherwise known as the perseverance of the saints. The combination of those two teachings leads many unbelievers to make a casual profession of faith, with the affirmation that they are saved immediately and always will be irrespective of how they live. Let's inspect Scripture to understand the trouble with this perspective.

Jesus said, "Unless your righteousness exceeds the righteousness of the scribes and Pharisees, you will by no means enter the kingdom of heaven" (Matthew 5:20). Was the wickedness of the scribes and Pharisees obvious to all who observed them in public? Did they profess hatred for or disinterest in God? Did the Pharisees' lives openly embrace sin? On the contrary, they were religious leaders who claimed to love God and outwardly appeared to follow His precepts. The Jewish community held them in high esteem and viewed them as the model for spiritual maturity. However, their hearts remained unchanged. They lived for themselves, not God. They valued status and appearance more than a genuine relationship with the Lord. They focused on religion instead of relationship because religion provided the temporal benefits they wanted.

The American church has adopted many of the behaviors, attitudes, and perspectives of the Pharisees. Too often we place greater importance on appearing religious than on cultivating a closer relationship with Christ. We concern ourselves more with going to church, saying the right things, and going through the motions of Christianity, than with living the radical life of discipleship Jesus describes. We need to recognize the parallels we share with the Pharisees and repent. Ask God to convict, convert, and change us so we model Jesus in our lives. If we continue to mirror the Pharisees, we will suffer the same judgment Jesus pronounced on them (see Luke 11:37-52 and Matthew 23:1-36).

What the Pharisees failed to understand was that a genuine relationship with God yields dramatic change in every facet of life. It leads to a life of sacrifice not excess, a life of service not pleasure. They believed professing faith in God and saying they loved Him proved their spiritual maturity. But it only proved they were religious. For them, faith evidenced itself in words. Declaring belief in God, claiming commitment to Him, and offering the right prayers were indisputable evidence of their faith. It did not matter that their hearts remained in rebellion and their lifestyles continued in wickedness. Claiming to know and obey God gave them a license to live in whatever manner they wanted, no matter how selfish, unmerciful, arrogant, or unkind their behavior.

The church at Laodicea shared the same misunderstanding. Its spiritual condition left it least likely to be used by God because it was neither bold for the gospel nor fully committed to the Lord. Its passion was not for the things above nor did it demonstrate a transformed life for Jesus. It was lukewarm. It claimed to love God but did not actually live for Him. Jesus informed it, "I know your works, that you are neither cold nor hot. I could wish you were cold or hot. So then, because you are lukewarm, and neither cold nor hot, I will spew you out of my mouth. Because you say, 'I am rich, have become wealthy, and have need of nothing'—and do not know that you are wretched, miserable, poor, blind, and naked" (Revelation 3:15-17).

The faith held by the Laodicean church focused on the outward. They said and believed the right things, appeared religious, and had confidence in their spiritual health. Unfortunately, on the inside they had never changed. They had not turned from sin or put to death their love for the world. That left the church lukewarm. They were blind to their need for God because they believed He was already in their midst. They failed to understand their need for a transformed life in Christ because they believed He had already transformed them. Their awareness of God kept them from being cold, but their superficial relationship with Him kept them from being hot. They were useless.

Magnifying its problem was that the Laodicean church viewed its spiritual condition through a temporal lens. They believed themselves spiritually healthy and mature because they were rich and had grown wealthy. They incorrectly assumed that possessing the world's goods evidenced their blessing by God. They mistakenly thought worldly success reflected God's approval. As a result, they held an inflated view of their spiritual maturity asserting, "I am rich, have become wealthy, and have need of nothing." They esteemed themselves so highly that they needed nothing, not even God.

The truth was nearly the opposite. God vehemently rejected the faith of the Laodicean church as disingenuous. He describes its faith in starkly unfavorable terms. He asserts that the church's faith left it wretched and miserable. Despite their worldly wealth, they were spiritually poor. And they were so distant from God that they were blind to the truth. They failed to see their true spiritual state. How could the church so dramatically misunderstand its spiritual condition? How could it fail to recognize how detached it was from the Lord? The church's failure stemmed from its emphasis on outward appearance and correlating temporal wealth with spiritual health.

Unfortunately, many of us adopt the same perspectives. We believe anyone making a verbal profession of faith in Jesus automatically becomes a Christian. In our minds, words reflect reality. Faith exists upon reciting the sinner's prayer, regardless of whether a lifestyle evidences faith. A life focused on self and this world does not discount the sincerity of faith. Lifestyles of sin reflect a back-slid Christian if he has professed trust in the Lord, not an indication of inauthentic faith.

But Jesus rebuked this perspective. Knowing how widespread this heretical view would become, Jesus offers numerous warnings that we not rely on our words as evidence of genuine faith. Since an inconsistency often exists between our words and our lifestyles, how do we determine what we really believe? Examine the heart, for it demonstrates the presence or absence of authentic faith. The heart reveals your true relationship with God, not the words you speak. Sadly, many who profess faith in Jesus eventually learn their faith was insincere. Like the Pharisees, they were religious but they were not the Lord's.

"Not everyone who says to me, 'Lord, Lord' shall enter the kingdom of heaven, but he who does the will of My Father in heaven. Many will say to Me in that day, 'Lord, Lord, have we not prophesied in Your name, cast out demons in Your name, and done many wonders in Your name?' And then I will declare to them, 'I never knew you, depart from Me, you who practice lawlessness'" (Matthew 7:21-23).

We need to absorb several important points from these verses because they refute what we learn in many churches. One widely shared view essentially affirms: "saying is believing." That is, proclaiming the name of Christ verifies belief in Christ; anyone acknowledging his trust in Jesus possesses authentic faith. But mere words do not make a Christian. Simply reciting a sinner's prayer or verbalizing love for Jesus does not substantiate one's faith. Jesus repudiates the belief that calling Him "Lord, Lord" demonstrates sincere faith. He specifically says that on Judgment Day many who call Him "Lord" will not enter the kingdom of heaven. On that day, countless people will realize their profession of faith in Jesus never led to salvation. Claiming faith in Christ never guaranteed them eternal life since they did not genuinely believe.

If simply verbalizing trust in Jesus and claiming He is Lord does not prove faith, what does? One must commit to Christ with his heart, mind, soul, and strength. His belief must flow from the heart rather than flow from the mouth, and a faith rooted in the heart impacts every area of life. The genuine believer holds back nothing in his commitment to Jesus. It does not hedge bets. It does not seek the minimum required by the Lord. It goes all-in. Belief from the heart transforms behavior.

Coming to Christ yields an entirely new person, who no longer possesses the vestiges of his former self. Paul explained that anyone who comes to Christ "is a new creation" in whom "old things have passed away" and "*all* things have become new (2 Corinthians 5:17, emphasis added). In contrast, verbal belief leaves areas of life untouched. An individual who commits to Christ in words alone retains many of his secret sins. He refuses to submit to Jesus as Lord in every way. He wants to maintain his current life and simply add Jesus to it.

This is the faith of easy-believism. It imposes few requirements from the person professing faith in God. It emphasizes the outward appearance of faith and verbalizes love and trust for Jesus. It ignores dozens of lessons Jesus taught regarding the life He calls His disciples to live. It views as irrelevant any passage of Scripture that makes life more difficult for the believer. Easy-believism simply wants to graft Christ into a selfish life with the expectation that He makes everything better for the believer. It wants all the benefits that Jesus brings without any of the "burdens" He imposes.

Distinguishing between genuine faith and easy-believism is as simple as identifying what each faith produces. Easy-believism produces casual and carnal Christians whose lives largely mirror those of the world. Authentic faith produces disciples living sacrificial lives. Easy-believism seeks its own, under the auspices of faith in Christ. Genuine faith seeks Jesus and His glory in all things. Easy-believism yields modest, superficial change in the life of its adherents. Sincere faith in the Lord results in complete transformation of the believer, his speech, thoughts, conduct, and lifestyle. Easy-believism revels in appearance, using religious language, and playing "church" while continuing to pursue its own agenda. Real faith delights in knowing the Lord, spending time in His presence, developing His attributes of humility and holiness, and implementing His agenda.

Surprisingly, I have heard many believers give testimonies stating very little changed after coming to faith in Christ. Maybe they grew up in a Christian family; perhaps they had a sense of morality at an early age. Whatever the reason, they lived "good lives" prior to becoming a Christian. As a result, they indicate their lives underwent minimal change upon accepting Jesus as Savior, just a little softening along the edges. What such testimonies fail to understand is that the most egregious sins are not drug abuse, alcoholism, violence, or some other easily observed act that even society recognizes as morally inappropriate. Those are byproducts of our sin. The egregious sins dwell in our hearts and are rebellion, unbridled selfishness, and pride. We need to repent from these sins and ask God to remove them from our hearts. As He does, every area of life transforms for the believer. More than the absence of glaring, outward sin, a believer's life evidences more and more the attributes of Christ. Increasingly, he reflects an unrestrained passion for Jesus, bringing Him glory in everything he does, and extending His good news to as many people as possible.

Sadly, too many of us have little interest in reaching the lost for Jesus. Too few of us have genuine passion for the Lord, evidenced by the time we spend with Him each day. Too many of us seek our own glory far more often than we seek His. Too few of us invest sacrificially in His work. Too many of us pursue selfish objectives that serve our own purposes while too few of us seek His will regardless of whether it aligns to our own. Our behavior and desires in such areas reveal the condition of our hearts, which reflect the [lack of] authenticity of our faith.

A genuine disciple of Jesus undergoes a spiritual "heart transplant." His passion, priorities, and perspective all change radically as they shift from a focus on self to a focus on the Lord. Have you undergone a spiritual heart transplant? Have your passions, priorities, and perspectives shifted from a focus on self to a focus on Jesus and His will? In determining if you have had a spiritual heart transplant, reflect on several questions:

- What upsets you more, the loss of countless souls to hell or the loss of your favorite team?

- What brings you more joy, your favorite entertainment or someone coming to faith in Jesus?

- When missions are discussed at church, are you bored, modestly interested, or enthusiastic?

- What excites you more, shopping at your favorite store or spending the day serving others?

- What motivates you more, getting a promotion or hearing the Lord say, "Well done"?

Of course this represents a small sample of the questions we can ask ourselves in gauging the sincerity of our faith, but these reflect the types of questions we should contemplate. If we seek guidance from the Holy Spirit, He will reveal where we place our allegiance, with "self" or with Jesus.

Returning to Matthew 7, Jesus informs us many will be surprised at His second coming because they "prophesied in [His] name" (vs. 23) yet He commands them to depart from His presence—presumably into the lake of fire. Pause for a moment and reflect on that statement, especially if you are a pastor, priest, Sunday school teacher, seminary professor, author, or Christian teacher. What does Jesus really say here? On Judgment Day, many of those who taught in His name will be cast from heaven and spend eternity in hell.

These are not teachers of Hinduism, Islamic leaders or Buddhist priests. They are Christian pastors who profess faith in Christ. They are instructors of the Christian faith who teach in Jesus' name. They are mainstream and evangelical influencers at all echelons of Christian leadership and across all denominations. Despite leading and teaching in Jesus' name, they are dispatched from His presence on Judgment Day.

While no one can know which Christian leaders possess authentic faith, we do know with certainty that some leaders have no genuine relationship with Jesus. If many Christian leaders have no real relationship with Christ, we ought to carefully consider the sincerity of our own faith lest we make the same mistake. The faux faith of many pastors and teachers points to the criticality of individually studying the Bible and allowing the Holy Spirit to reveal God's Word and truth. Confirm your pastor's message aligns with Scripture. Never assume a Christian leader speaks truth unless you validate with Scripture.

So why does Jesus cast so many professing Christians from His presence on Judgment Day? What kept them from entering eternity with the Lord? The answer, Jesus tells us, is that they never knew Him. That does not mean they never knew Jesus intellectually, nor knew about Him, nor knew who He was historically. Their problem was they *only* knew Jesus in an intellectual and historical manner. They knew a great deal *about* Him but never knew Him personally. They had no relationship with Him nor had a passion to draw near to Him. They never knew Him in their heart. Theirs was a sanitized, distant knowledge of Jesus, not a personal, intimate relationship with Him. The former claim a love for Jesus and profess Him as Lord, but no change occurs in the heart. In contrast, the latter are born again into a new life that overflows with sacrificial love, commitment, and obedience.

God designed us to know Him. More than anything, experiencing God daily and personally leads to a life filled with value and meaning.

Absent a vibrant relationship with the Lord, we never become the individuals God intended. Each person is at his best when developing a closer and more meaningful relationship with Jesus. Take a minute to reflect on your relationship in Christ. Do you know Him on a personal level? Do you spend regular and substantive time together? Are you learning more about His attributes and character, and in the process becoming more like Him? Unless you have a personal relationship with Jesus, the rest of the book offers you no value. Everything we discuss in the remaining chapters builds on the foundation of Christ. We identify the life Jesus calls His followers to live and challenge each other to apply in our lives the difficult truths He shared with His disciples.

But it all begins with Jesus. Getting everything else right in the book is useless unless it brings the reader closer to God. In fact, without the presence of the Holy Spirit no one will make it through the rest of the book. The Holy Spirit will reveal God's truth, convict us where we have sin, and strengthen us to understand and apply the truth we examine in each chapter. The primary purpose of this book is to challenge each believer to grow in His relationship with Jesus and become more like Him. That way, none of us hears Him say, "I never knew you."

================= QUESTIONS: =================

1. How can someone profess Jesus as Lord or teach in His name yet not have an authentic faith?

2. How does a sincere faith evidence itself in the life of a believer?

3. Does your life reflect a personal, growing relationship with Christ, or a casual familiarity about Him? If the latter, what keeps you from committing your life to Him entirely?

If you confess with your mouth the Lord Jesus and believe in your heart that God has raised Him from the dead, you will be saved. For with the heart one believes to righteousness and with the mouth confession is made to salvation.

—Romans 10:9-10

CHAPTER 2

Authentic Belief

Perhaps more than any other Scripture, these verses crystallize the problem crippling the church today. The verses form the basis for distinguishing between a faux faith that sounds good and a sincere faith that embraces the difficult truths Jesus taught. The former deceives the heart and leads to destruction while the latter transforms lives and leads to salvation.

Paul identifies two requirements of faith in these verses. First, you must confess Jesus as Lord. By verbalizing your allegiance you affirm Him as ruler of your life. God requires each believer to make a public profession of faith so others know of his commitment to Christ. Jesus calls no one to live a secret faith. For most Americans, this represents the easier of the two requirements. National surveys consistently find 60 to 80 percent of Americans claim Christianity as their religion (see http://religions.pewforum.org/reports) and there are tens of thousands of churches across the country filled with people who claim Jesus as Lord. While doctrine varies widely between churches, they share the belief that Christ is Savior and most of their parishioners insist they love God.

But if we are a majority Christian nation, why do so many of our citizens live a decidedly unchristian life? What explains the divide between a nation professing Jesus as Lord yet focusing relentlessly on self? How can our nation declare its commitment to God but simultaneously demonstrate idolatry for this world? How can so many churchgoers assert their allegiance to Christ while having affairs, purveying pornography, clinging to bitterness, and living lifestyles of sin? Why do so many verbalize a love for God but spend so little time with Him and His word? How do so many of us say yes to Jesus but no to the hard lessons He taught?

The answer to these questions lies in the second half of verse nine. You must believe in your heart that Jesus is Lord. Professing faith alone is insufficient. In fact, the Old Testament offers numerous examples of people who professed their love for God but whose hearts remained uncommitted to Him. Jesus quoted Isaiah in describing such people: "These people draw near to Me with their mouth, and honor Me with their lips, but their heart is far from Me, and in vain they worship Me, teaching as doctrines the commandments of men" (Matthew 15:8-9). Jesus labeled as hypocrites those who practice such faith. The one who draws near to God in word but not in his heart holds no real faith. Too many of us fall into this trap. We praise God on Sunday mornings, pray at church, and tell others how much we love God, but our hearts are far from Him. Our worship, prayers, and professions of faith are in vain because we never surrendered our heart to Him. Our faith comprises lots of religious words but no changed heart.

Paul emphasizes the criticality of the heart in the faith equation. Professing Christ as Lord does not provide salvation unless it accompanies a belief from the heart. A profession-based faith, absent the heart, is no faith at all. It is showmanship. It flows from a wicked heart and seeks its own purposes. That explains how many Americans can profess faith in Jesus yet live such selfish, arrogant, and worldly lives. They do not genuinely believe Jesus nor have they earnestly committed their lives to Him. Proverbs underscores the importance of the heart in demonstrating genuine faith; it tells us, "a man's heart reveals the man" (Proverbs 27:19).

Returning to verse ten in Romans, Paul says that "with the heart one believes to righteousness." Genuine faith impacts the heart and leads to a lifestyle of righteousness. Any believer whose life does not grow in righteousness does not truly believe. Sincere faith always leads to a life that grows to resemble Jesus more and more. Faux faith always leads to a life that continues to mirror our unsaved friends and neighbors.

One of the great challenges the church faces in a majority Christian nation is encouraging its adherents to believe with the heart and not just confess with the mouth. Once Christianity becomes a nation's dominant religion, as in America, it becomes culturally appropriate to say you are a Christian. Claiming faith in Christ often allows businessmen to connect with more customers who want to do business with a fellow believer. Moreover, many people hold the perspective that to be American is to be Christian. It is essentially part of the cultural fabric of our country. Not surprising, these people live as cultural Christians.

Ask an American Christian his basis for faith and you hear a lot of different things. Some attribute their faith to how they were raised, others to their parents baptizing them as infants, and still others because they believe Jesus is God. It turns out that many Americans base their Christian faith on something other than a personal relationship with Jesus Christ. They point to lots of externalities that affirm their faith, but never mention a changed heart.

Jesus highlighted this distinction when addressing the Pharisees, who excelled at professing faith in God and honoring Him with their words. He said to them, "You are those who justify yourselves before men, but God knows your hearts" (Luke 16:15). While the Pharisees appeared godly and righteous before men, their hearts overflowed with pride and selfishness. Observers were fooled by the Pharisees' words and appearance. Jesus, however, knew the condition of their hearts. He was not fooled.

Similarly, many of us fool one another with our perfect church attendance, robust singing during worship, and spiritual-sounding prayers. But unless our heart believes, our faith mirrors the Pharisees'. Our verbiage does not fool God. He knows the genuine condition of the heart. And lest we confidently presume the purity of our faith, remember that the Pharisees thought they possessed genuine faith as well. It was not as if they knew their faith was disingenuous. They earnestly believed they obeyed God and honored Him with their hearts. The same holds true for most of us; I doubt any of us knowingly give God lip service and withhold our heart. Yet a great many of us do, revealing an absence of authentic faith.

Jesus emphasizes this point when counseling the Pharisees on what defiles a man. He informs them that "whatever enters a man from outside cannot defile him, because it does not enter his heart" (Mark 7:18b-19a). The heart reveals the validity of a believer's faith and impacts his life. If his heart embraces Jesus as Lord, then he brings each area of his life into alignment with the commands of God. On the other hand, the life of a man with insincere faith imitates the world. Little in his life reflects God's will. Continuing, Jesus observes that "from within, out of the heart of men, proceed evil thoughts, adulteries, fornications, murders, thefts, covetousness, wickedness, deceit, licentiousness, an evil eye, blasphemy, pride, foolishness. All these things come from within and defile a man" (Mark 7:21-23). Our behavior, thoughts and speech reveal the condition of our heart and demonstrate what we really believe.

Your obedience to God also validates the authenticity of your faith. Do you keep His commands? John advises us that "we know that we know Him, if we keep His commandments. He who says, 'I know Him,' and does not keep His commandments is a liar, and the truth is not in him . . . He who says he abides in Him ought himself also to walk just as He walked" (1 John 2:3-4, 6). You profess faith in God but remain unsure whether your belief leaps from the heart or simply reflects lip service. John explains how we identify sincere faith. We know Jesus personally if we keep His commandments. That obedience reflects a changed heart, a heart that believes. Distinguishing between professed faith and actual belief, John identifies those who claim to know Jesus but do not obey His commands. Anyone fitting this description "is a liar, and the truth is not in him." To avoid confusion about the legitimacy of such a person's faith, John uses very direct language. Any individual who says he is a Christian but lives life in disobedience to God is a hypocrite. He does not have an authentic faith. He is a liar and his claim of knowing Jesus is a lie as well. Some readers may balk at such pointed remarks but John wanted no room for ambiguity. His depicts such people as liars to emphasize they had a fraudulent faith. In doing so he hopes to keep others from making the same mistake.

Notice that John does not qualify our obedience. He does not suggest we are Christ's if we keep some of His commands, or even most of His commands. Nor does John indicate we are the Lord's if we obey the commands with which we agree, or at least the ones that are not difficult. Instead, John tells us we know Jesus as Lord "if we keep His commandments." We do not get to pick and choose which ones to keep. John also informs us that if we genuinely abide in Christ we ought to walk as He walked. Examine your life and compare it to Jesus'. Are they similar? Do you share His passions? Do you maintain the same priorities in your life that He exemplified in His? Do you mirror His love for all people, especially those rejected, hurting, and broken? Do you invest your life in the same things He invested His— discipling others and knowing the Father more closely? If not, the truth may not be in you.

We spend the remainder of the book examining the commands Jesus gave His disciples. He expects us to obey them as we submit to His Lordship. In doing so we not only serve as a light to the world, we demonstrate the authenticity of our faith. You will learn that many of His commands are difficult to obey because they go against our sin nature. For this reason, you may find it valuable to have an accountability partner so you sharpen each other's faith as iron sharpens iron (see Proverbs 27:17). Keep in mind that if we claim to know Jesus but do not keep His commands, we are "a liar, and the truth is not in [us]", which includes disobeying or ignoring the challenging and uncomfortable commands.

======================== QUESTIONS: ========================

1. Why is a verbal profession of faith insufficient in demonstrating true belief in Jesus?

2. Paul tells us sincere faith comes from the heart. Does your faith arise from your heart? How do you know?

3. John says that if we abide in Christ, we should walk as He walked? Describe Jesus' walk—think in terms of His priorities, actions, attributes, focus. How closely does your walk mirror Jesus'?

PART II

Difficult because: We Must Die to Live

Our sin nature possesses tremendous power. It influences all areas of our lives and always in a way that serves its purpose. It relentlessly demands our obedience and does not tolerate resistance. It deceives us to achieve its objectives and impose its will on us. Every evil thought, selfish decision, hateful word, and act of iniquity proceeds from our sin nature, our "flesh" as the Bible describes it.

As powerful as our sin nature is, it exercises no power over the Spirit of God. Whenever the Spirit battles the flesh, the Spirit always wins. God gives us His Spirit when we come to faith in Jesus. He equips us with the power to overcome the flesh that rages in us. He empowers us to conquer our sin nature and reject the path of wickedness. While we do not, as believers, always win our individual battles with our sin nature, we should win an increasing number of them. We win more and more of them when we follow the flesh less and less. This occurs when we crucify the desires of our flesh and put to death our sin nature.

Implementing these practices daily is an extremely difficult challenge. Our flesh fights us and employs every resource available to stop us from obeying the Lord. Once we put our flesh on notice that we no longer serve it but Jesus instead, it will tempt, lure, and entice us with sin. It will seek our return to selfish ways, exercising treachery and pretense to convince us the call of Christ is a sham and discipleship does not require its death. So we must take up this battle daily against our sin nature.

This likely represents the most difficult part of the Christian faith but every genuine disciple does so.

In this section we examine what Jesus and His apostles say about our sin nature and how we address it once we submit to Him. We learn the emphasis Jesus places on dying to self. We investigate Scripture that captures the expectations Jesus has for everyone who commits to Him as a disciple, and learn to count the cost of being a believer (because the cost is significant). This cost does not represent payment for redemption and salvation; we know those are a free gift of God. The cost represents our sacrifice for Jesus because of the redemption and salvation His grace provides. Scripture does not equivocate on these truths; it consistently reinforces this message across all four gospel accounts and all the epistles.

In the next six chapters we study biblical passages that leave no room for confusion or doubt on how the life of every believer changes if he has authentic faith. Keep in mind that as you read these chapters your flesh will seek to deceive you from the truth and convince you your faith does not require obeying Jesus' commands. Lean heavily on the Holy Spirit to confirm His truth.

If anyone desires to come after Me, let him deny himself,
and take up his cross daily, and follow Me.

—Luke 9:23

CHAPTER 3

Deny Yourself

Jesus outlined a challenging path for those who would follow Him as a disciple and profess Him as Lord. He identifies three actions for becoming His disciple.

First: Deny yourself. Seems easy enough, right? Most Christians would argue they deny themselves to some degree in many areas of life. But Jesus' challenge does not cover a limited part of our lives, nor does it apply on an intermittent basis. He does not command us to gradual, modest change in denying ourselves. His call to deny our "self" represents a wholesale change in philosophy. We transition from a life in which we put our interests, desires, and priorities first to one that places Him first in each of those areas.

His challenge is comprehensive. We are not to retain hidden desires, secret ambitions, or an unrelinquished interest. Moreover, His call requires more than just putting Him first in each area of life, it necessitates we eliminate entirely our own agenda in these areas. We do not get there overnight but must exercise discipline in denying "self" in every way including our:

- Passions
- Focus
- Agenda
- Priorities

- Aspirations
- Relationships
- Income
- Time

Denying "self" in each area is difficult. We set-aside our passions and ambitions and replace them with a desire to implement God's will entirely in our lives. We refuse to create our own agenda, choosing instead to understand and embrace God's approach in each situation. We give our hopes and dreams over to the Lord, not asking Him to fulfill them but to replace them with His purpose for our lives. Many readers will object to giving up their hopes and dreams because the church has taught that God wants them to realize those hopes and dreams. But His word is clear—we must deny "self" to become His disciple and that includes whatever goals we have for our lives (keep in mind that the life He has planned for you exceeds in every way the plan you have for yourself).

What does denying self really mean, in simple terms? Basically, it means acting selflessly. Our natural tendency as sinful people is to behave selfishly, in our relationships with others, in how we invest our time, in how we spend money, in our interactions with God. We prioritize our interests first and only consider God and others after that. But a disciple of Christ learns to set aside his interests entirely. Instead, he considers the desires of God first and the needs and wellbeing of others second. His interests do not come third or even last; he fully denies them so they cease to exist.

Understanding, accepting, and implementing this truth is impossible without grace and power from the Holy Spirit. We are selfish by nature and do not easily acquiesce to God's will in this area. Behaving selflessly likely results in our not getting what we want. That is why we must give up completely our wants and desires. Until we do, we will feel like we received the short end of the deal. However, when we surrender to God our interests, ambitions, agenda, and dreams, we do not concern ourselves with whether we come out ahead in any circumstance. We find satisfaction in obeying and bringing glory to the Lord.

When we look at the sin that consumes this world, selfishness is almost always at the root. That sin leads people to harm others emotionally, physically, and financially. Selfishness leads to heinous crimes like murder, domestic abuse, and rape; it leads to destructive behaviors like substance abuse, buying more than you can afford, and becoming a workaholic; it leads to inappropriate conduct such as rudeness, arrogance, and disrespect. Selfishness destroys more lives and separates more people from a relationship with God than probably any other sin.

In contrast, Jesus modeled a selfless life. Read through the gospels and you will observe Him continually prioritizing the Father. He frequently sought the Father in prayer (Matthew 14:23) and had studied the Torah thoroughly enough to quote from it regularly (See Mark 11:17; 12:36; Matthew 15:8-9; 21:42). He focuses tirelessly on other people. The gospel authors recount example after example of Jesus meeting the needs of others whose paths He crossed: allowing the little kids to come to Him (Luke 18:15-17), talking with the gentile woman whose daughter He healed (see Mark 7:24-30), forgiving a woman broken by sin (Luke 7:36-50), and healing the diseased (see Mark 1:40-41; Luke 8:43-48; Luke 13:10-13; Matthew 8:28-32; Matthew 9:18-34).

We need to follow Jesus' example of a selfless life. It will not happen by accident. You must purpose to deny self. Take substantive action in at least a couple areas. Two good places to start are relationships and time. Identify opportunities each day to serve the people you encounter, whether friends or strangers. Ask God to make you sensitive to the needs of others. Consider encounters with the hurting and broken as opportunities to be Jesus to them rather than disruptive events that inconvenience you. Ask Him for a heart that shows compassion, love, and kindness to those you meet each day, and not just see them as a clerk, a waitress, a bank teller, or a salesman. Treat them as Jesus would, not as a speed bump on your way to accomplishing your errands for the day.

Second: Take up your cross daily. What did the cross represent with Jesus? It reflected complete obedience to God no matter the cost. It glorified God. It acknowledged that the will of God was best, even when not understanding it fully. It demonstrated that a focus on people matters, especially a compassionate concern for their souls. How do we take up the cross daily?

- Take up that which glorifies God.
- Take up humility.
- Take up serving others.
- Take up gentleness.
- Take up loving people.
- Take up extreme generosity.
- Take up mercy.
- Take up holiness.
- Take up extended prayer.
- Take up a mission orientation.
- Take up an eternal focus.

Jesus encourages us to take up the cross daily. Pursue those actions that demonstrate obedience to God every day. Embed them as part of your daily routine so they become habits. Developing habits require diligence and effort. You do not become an obedient Christian by chance. Consider other areas in life where you enjoy success. Did you achieve a level of ongoing, sustained achievement by irregular effort and half-hearted commitment? I doubt it. Likely hard work, focused effort, and unrelenting resilience played a big role. Similarly, you must dedicate yourself to obedience in order to establish it as a consistent part of your daily life.

Third: Follow Jesus. This seems straightforward enough, and most Christians would assert they already follow Jesus. But do we really follow Him? Do we follow Him in all things or do we hold back parts of our life? Do we follow Him when it is difficult and perhaps overwhelming, or do we merely go through the motions to appear Christian? Do we follow Him joyfully, or reluctantly and begrudgingly? Do we follow Jesus because we love Him or merely out of a sense of obligation?

So what does following the Lord mean? It means going where He went and doing what He did. He went to people, especially the hurting, rejected, discouraged, and hopeless. He met their needs, served them, shared truth with them, demonstrated substantive love to them, and pointed them to a relationship with God. He cared about people and their needs—physical, emotional, and most of all spiritual. Similarly, we need to go to people, especially "the least of these", and meet their needs. We must prioritize people in our lives, ahead of our own plans and agenda. We not only follow Jesus in doing so, we reflect the truth of what it means to claim Him as Lord.

So how often do pastors preach on the denial of self and taking up our cross daily? How frequently do we hear a sermon on daily denying our selfish ways as a biblical response to Jesus' command for His disciples? It is too rare a message; rare in part because it is unpopular in the church and in part because too few of us actually believe it. Too often we believe genuine faith allows us to maintain a focus on self.

But the two views are polar opposites. On one hand, Jesus calls us to deny ourselves in order to follow Him; the culture, on the other hand, lifts up "self" and celebrates it. Too many in the church want to integrate these into a hybrid option that allows disciples of Jesus to remain faithful to self while also serving God. But that option does not exist; it is impossible to implement. You cannot blend the call of Christ with the celebration of self. Our "self" reflects our sin nature and it wars with God. It desires lordship of our life and wants to control our decisions. Our "flesh" has no interest in abdicating its authority to Jesus. That is why Jesus said we must deny ourselves to be His disciple. He will not reside with anyone desiring two lords. You must choose. If unwilling to deny yourself, then you cannot be His disciple.

Paul reinforced this point in his letter to the church at Corinth, remarking that Jesus "died for all, that those who live should live no longer for themselves but for Him who died for them and rose again" (2 Corinthians 5:15). Jesus' death does not enable us to continue living for ourselves. He did not bear the brutality of the Roman soldiers so we could continue pursuing our own agenda in life. He did not suffer barbaric torture from His culture so we could chase our lusts for this world. He died for all, but He died that we might die ourselves; not a physical death but a death unto our flesh and sin nature. In accepting the sacrificial death of Jesus as atonement for our sin, He calls us to live for Him. In essence, anyone who desires to come after Him must deny himself.

Jesus indicates that sorrow awaits those who elevate self and pursue its desires. Those who prioritize selfish pursuits eventually experience judgment. He warns, "But woe to you who are rich, for you have received your consolation. Woe to you who are full, for you shall hunger. Woe to you who laugh now, for you shall mourn and weep. Woe to you when all men speak well of you, for so did their fathers to the false prophets" (Luke 6:24-26).

These verses do not indict anyone who makes money, enjoys a hearty meal, has a good laugh, or is held in high esteem. Rather, it implies that those who pursue a selfish lifestyle of wealth, pleasure, satisfaction and worldly approval will face considerable pain and suffering in the world to come. They chose to fulfill their selfish desires and pursue selfish priorities instead of adopting a pattern of denying self. In this life they enjoy momentary happiness, but they suffer woe in the age to come.

Understand that believers do not deny self to earn Jesus' approval. He calls us to deny self because we cannot fully follow Him when we focus on our own agenda. By daily choosing to set aside our plans and seek His instead, we make ourselves available for His use. In contrast, when we pursue our own will, the cares of this world invariably distract us and we never fulfill God's plan. That so many of us mistakenly believe our will and the Lord's will are "one in the same" highlights our shallow understanding of discipleship. The call of Christ is a call to deny self and put Him first.

Paul issued a similar challenge, encouraging us to "put on the Lord Jesus Christ and make no provision for the flesh, to fulfill its lusts" (Romans 13:14). When we prioritize our career, success, comfort, pleasure, reputation, and wealth, we demonstrate selfishness. Pursuing the agenda of self precludes putting on the Lord Jesus. Do not deceive yourself and think you can enjoy the benefits of selfish behavior yet adhere to the call of Jesus. The voice in your head may tell you "nonsense" and suggest you can follow Jesus *and* live a lifestyle of selfishness. Do not embrace that view. That is your sin nature. It wants you to compromise and retain a selfish lifestyle, even if it costs you your soul.

You must decide whether to believe Jesus or "self." If you choose to follow Jesus, you must deny yourself. You must take up your cross daily, which reveals a spirit of obedience to God and His commands. If you follow Jesus, then follow His example. Follow His priorities, follow His passions, and follow His agenda. And in each of those areas, deny yourself.

================================ QUESTIONS: ================================

1. In learning to deny "self," we must include every aspect of our lives. Ask the Holy Spirit to reveal what it means in the following areas:

   • Your relationships: parents, spouse, kids, colleagues, neighbors, strangers.

   • Your income.

   • Your career.

   • Your time.

   • Your reputation.

- Your lifestyle.

- Your priorities.'

- Your dreams.

2. How do we serve God when we deny self?

3. Jesus denied Himself when He took up His cross and made His way to Golgotha that Friday morning. He denied Himself when He allowed the Roman guards to beat Him. He denied Himself when He suffered an unbelievable death. How does Jesus' example of denying Himself, in obedience to God, encourage you to deny yourself for Him as His disciple?

Knowing that a man is not justified by the works of the law but by faith in Jesus Christ, even we have believed in Christ Jesus, that we might be justified by faith in Christ and not by the works of the law; for by the works of the law no flesh shall be justified. But if, while we seek to be justified by Christ, we ourselves are found to be sinners, is Christ therefore a minister of sin? Certainly not! For if I build again those things which I have destroyed, I make myself a transgressor. For I through the law died to the law that I might live to God. I have been crucified with Christ; it is no longer I who live, but Christ lives in me; and the life which I now live in the flesh I live by faith in the Son of God, who loved me and gave Himself for me. I do not set aside the grace of God; for if righteousness comes through the law, then Christ died in vain.

—Galatians 2:16-21

CHAPTER 4

Crucified with Christ

This passage reinforces the truth that salvation comes by faith and not from our works. Paul begins the passage observing that "a man is not justified by the works of the law but by faith in Jesus Christ," and concludes the passage asserting that Christ need not have died if salvation comes from the law. Paul wanted the early church to understand clearly that no one achieves salvation on his own. No amount of effort, no amount of obedience, no amount of good works earns an individual eternal life with God. This perspective represented a significant change from other faiths of that time, whereby people had to work their way to heaven. Paul exercised considerable care in communicating that faith in Christ provides the only path to salvation.

Continuing, Paul emphasizes the equally important truth that anyone placing his faith in Jesus no longer retains dominion over his life. Paul informs the church at Galatia, "I have been crucified with Christ; it is no longer I who live, but Christ who lives in me" (Galatians 2:20). Anyone who comes to Christ no longer lives for himself; he concedes his life for the Lord and for His will alone. He crucifies his life unto Christ. The sinner who recognizes the magnitude of God's mercy joyfully yields all authority of his life to God. His gratefulness to Jesus for restoring his relationship with God necessarily results in his abdicating all rights and control he has on his life.

This does not represent Christian theory. It is not a conceptual exercise that mandates your affirmation. It does not require mere intellectual recognition that you are crucified with Christ. It reflects the genuine perspective held by all true believers in Jesus. In accepting Him as Savior, you accept His physical death as a substitution for the spiritual death you deserve for your sins. You embrace His sacrifice as the atonement God requires for your sin. His physical crucifixion and resurrection provides eternal life for all who believe.

However, anyone who believes must himself be "crucified"—not physically but unto his flesh. Each believer must crucify his sin nature in response to the salvation God gives him. Every genuine believer crucifies himself unto Jesus for the glory of God. It reflects a response from each Christian who knows that but for the grace of God he would spend eternity in hell. Understanding the enormity of the sacrifice Jesus made compels every saint to willingly and joyfully sacrifice his life and aspirations for the Lord. He puts to death the lusts and desires that represent the old self, and replaces them with the holiness and righteousness of Jesus.

The entirety of your remaining physical life focuses on Jesus not yourself, if you are indeed His. Paul remarks that we "through the law died to the law that [we] might live to God" (Galatians 2:19). Do you see the dual truths contained in that verse? Yes, we no longer remain under the law when we come to Christ. But that does not release us to live in whatever manner we choose. Rather, we are called to live for God. We are driven to know Him more and more each day. We passionately seek to adopt His ways as our own. We put aside our will and replace it with His good and perfect will, even though it is unattractive to our sin nature. We do this gladly because He is our Lord.

We sacrifice to Him all our rights, privileges, and entitlements in this world, even as He did the same for us two thousand years ago. We cede all authority over our life. We abdicate our purpose, plans, and position to Him. The prism through which we see life's choices is the mind of Christ. No longer do we make decisions based on what is best for ourselves but on what best glorifies the Lord. We no longer seek to advance our agenda but seek to implement His.

As we learned in the previous chapter, this impacts every area of life including your career, relationships, investments, and your time. He liberates you in each area through your crucifying the flesh. No longer are you chained to the demands of the flesh, trying to accomplish the goals it establishes for you. The expectations of others no longer burden you, as you need not impress them or secure their approval. No more must you subject yourself to the demanding and wearying definitions of achievement and success instituted by your flesh and by others.

Now you need only obey the Lord. Your life's purpose is simple: knowing Him and sharing His love with others. How liberating. Obedience defines success; you need not worry about delivering any success in the path He sends you down. You trust Him for the outcomes. He does not demand specific results in your life since He and the Holy Spirit are responsible for those. He only asks that you obey.

It is unbiblical to suggest someone can place his faith in Jesus and still live for himself. To accept Jesus as Lord by necessity requires that he no longer operate as master of his own destiny. He transitions all ownership and title to his life to Jesus. In essence, he becomes a slave to Christ. The idea that one can come to Jesus' feet, accept the grace and mercy He offers, and not crucify his "flesh" has no basis in Scripture. That thought implies that salvation imposes no cost. God's Word teaches that it cost Jesus everything on earth to provide us the free gift of salvation, and it costs us everything once we receive the gift of eternal life.

You may bristle and insist that sounds a lot like a works-based salvation. But that is not the case. Paul understood that salvation by grace went hand in hand with having to give all once we receive that gift. We read earlier his instruction that "a man is not justified by the works of the law but by faith in Jesus Christ . . . for by the works of the law no flesh shall be justified" (Galatians 2:16). Paul emphasizes the fact that salvation comes by grace alone. He asserts that truth throughout his epistles.

But grace received always results in the recipient crucifying the flesh. Paul tells the Galatians that "those who are Christ's have crucified the flesh, with its passions and desires" (Galatians 5:24). Paul does not recommend the death of self as an option for those who come to Jesus. Rather, he describes a certainty. Anyone who follows Jesus as a disciple will crucify the flesh; there are no exceptions. By crucifying the flesh, a believer puts to death those worldly passions and desires he pursued prior to placing his faith in Jesus. The challenge confronting anyone who names Jesus as Lord is not whether he crucifies his sin nature, but whether his faith is authentic. Genuine faith always results in crucified flesh. Always! A true believer shifts from living for self to living for God. Anyone who claims faith in Jesus but continues to live for himself possesses a faux faith.

How does someone crucify the flesh? He puts to death the "old man" of his sin nature. Scripture teaches "that our old man was crucified with Him, that the body of sin might be done away with, that we should no longer be slaves of sin" (Romans 6:6). In coming to Jesus and committing to Him as Lord, our flesh (the old man) is crucified. Sin no longer has dominion over us; we submit ourselves as slaves of Jesus instead. We dethrone the flesh from control and rule of our lives. We no longer pursue the career we want but the one the Lord wants for us—and it is possibly quite different. We do not pursue a sterling reputation among colleagues at work, with neighbors, or with our circle of friends. Instead, we pursue a reputation that honors the Lord and results in His approval as a "good and faithful servant." We devote our free time to developing our relationship with Jesus and not in satisfying our flesh. Instead of chasing short-term pleasure, we invest in activities that drive eternal value.

While the sacrificed activities will vary by person, as will the new activities each believer pursues, a dramatic change occurs in how the believer spends his time once he submits to Jesus. This happens because his former conduct was driven by the lusts of the flesh, whereas his new behavior is driven by a desire to know God. Even former activities that were not sinful on the surface arose from a sin nature that sought to be entertained, pleasured, and satisfied. On becoming a new creation, the believer puts aside those selfish pursuits and replaces them with a pursuit of God's will.

Paul reminds us that "you also reckon yourselves to be dead indeed to sin, but alive to God in Christ Jesus our Lord. Therefore do not let sin reign in your mortal body that you should obey it in its lusts" (Romans 6:11-12). In crucifying the flesh we now consider ourselves dead to sin. We do not seek that behavior which marked our prior life. We recognize that sin compromises our relationship with the Lord and so we avoid it. We understand that the new life we have, we have in Christ who makes us alive to God. Consequently, we seek a life that mirrors His. We remove sin from the throne of our heart and refuse to allow the flesh to reign in our lives. No longer is it our king that we should obey its orders. We refuse to follow its commands to pursue wicked conduct. We resist its efforts to tempt us into fulfilling its desires.

Why does Jesus call us to crucify the flesh? In doing so we more effectively follow His will and bear fruit for the kingdom. He informed His followers that "unless a grain of wheat falls into the ground and dies it remains alone; but if it dies it produces much grain. He who loves his life will lose it, and he who hates his life in this world will keep it for eternal life. If anyone serves Me, let him follow Me; and where I am there My servant will be also" (John 12:24-26).

By crucifying our flesh we die to self. It is in that dying that God uses us. Dying to self makes us available for the work He wants to accomplish in the world. We become fruitful, and our lives have an eternal impact on those around us. Jesus makes it clear, though, that He does not use those who remain alive to self. It is only the grain that dies which produces more grain. It is only the believer who crucifies his flesh who bears kingdom fruit.

Notice that Jesus warned that those who never die to self eventually die for eternity. Refusing to die to the flesh indicates an individual loves his life. He declines to yield to the Lord. Consequently, he loses his life in the world to come. He trades eternity with God for his right to live unto himself in this life. In contrast, he who "hates" his life in this world and counts himself dead to the flesh enjoys eternity with the Lord.

Jesus represents our example in dying to self. He put aside any personal interests He had and submitted Himself fully to the will of His Father. Peter reminds us that He "Himself bore our sins in His own body on the tree, that we, having died to sins, might live for righteousness—by whose stripes you were healed" (1 Peter 2:24). His selflessness restored our relationship with the Father. He sacrificed Himself on that tree that we might live for righteousness, not for ourselves. We have died to our sin nature if indeed we have submitted to Him as Lord.

1. Why does the believer crucify the flesh when he accepts Jesus as Lord?

2. How does the death of "self" evidence itself in the believer's life? How does your life reflect it?

3. In what area(s) of your life have you refused to crucify the flesh? Why do you retain control of that part of your life? What must you do to obey God in this?

For the *grace* of God that brings salvation has appeared to all men, *teaching* us that, *denying* ungodliness and worldly lusts, we should *live* soberly, righteously, and godly in the present age, *looking for* the blessed hope and glorious appearing of our great God and Savior Jesus Christ, who gave Himself for us, that He might *redeem* us from every lawless deed and *purify* for Himself His own people, *zealous for* good works.

—Titus 2:11-14, emphasis added

CHAPTER 5

Grace Teaches

Grace represents an awesome concept. God provides redemption from sin despite our unbridled wickedness. He offers forgiveness despite an absence of merit on our part. We have access to eternal life through the sacrifice of Jesus, who bridges the gap between our sin-stained lives and the holiness of God's presence. Grace yields salvation entirely as a result of God's mercy and nothing we do ourselves. Yet we must embrace that grace to receive it. God will not impose His grace on the disinterested person; He will not force anyone to accept His mercy.

While God extends His grace without requiring any effort on our part, that grace invariably impacts our lives. God does not offer grace so we can continue down the path of iniquity. His grace does not cover our sin so we can continue in a lifestyle of sin. He provides grace so we might have restored fellowship with Him. Grace teaches us several things according to Paul.

First, grace teaches we must deny ungodliness and worldly lusts in our lives. God abhors sin. He will not tolerate it in His presence. If we embrace God's grace but maintain a life of iniquity and wicked behavior, we fail to understand the purpose for which grace operates. We incorrectly view grace primarily as a vehicle to provide eternal life. We focus on our benefit (salvation) rather than God's purpose (restored fellowship). When grace genuinely exists in the life of a believer, he denies himself the sinful behavior and worldly conduct which he followed before coming to the Lord. When we truly understand the magnitude of God's love and the sacrifice His grace represents, we diligently turn from our sinful nature and seek His standard of holiness. We desire to live as He does—without worldly lusts or unrighteousness. Take a moment to consider whether this statement reflects your life. Do you seek to eliminate ungodliness and worldly lusts in the following areas?

- Gossip.
- Materialism.
- Pride.
- Idolatry.
- Idleness.
- Covetousness.
- Judgmental attitude.
- Uncaring.

Second, grace teaches and leads to a life that is "sober, righteous, and godly in the present age" (Titus 2:12). While God's grace is free, it produces a life with replaced priorities. No longer does the one who embraced grace live in wickedness. Instead he receives instruction from grace to live a life that is both righteous and godly. He receives this guidance with joy because he knows a more godly life honors the Lord and enhances his fellowship with God.

For example, a godly and righteous life avoids all sexual sins—any sex outside a biblical based marriage. In fact, believers avoid any behavior that leads to such sin. If single, a believer should resist intimate physical contact that often leads to sexual acts, including inappropriate petting and stroking. Even non-sexual behavior is dangerous when it excites or stimulates a person's sexual urges, since that often leads to sexual activity or contact. Avoid situations where such conduct naturally occurs; for example don't watch television in bed with your significant other. If married, do not flirt with someone other than your spouse, or invest in emotional or intellectual intimacy with someone other than your spouse. Maintain a healthy distance from the opposite sex in such areas to avoid developing improper feelings or urges. The godly and righteous life recognizes that avoiding sexual sin starts with eliminating temptation. Believers should also avoid inappropriate websites where sexually explicit material exists. If unable to resist such temptation, implement controls to prevent accessing them, such as having a spouse or friend install filtering software that prevents access. While potentially embarrassing, the believer understands it is more important to avoid sin and refrain from wicked behavior than appear righteous to friends and family.

Peter reminds us to "rest our hope fully upon the grace that is to be brought to you at the revelation of Jesus Christ; as obedient children, not conforming yourselves to the former lusts, as in your ignorance; but as He who called you is holy, you also be holy in all your conduct" (1 Peter 1:13b-15). Grace produces holiness in every believer's life. Sexual purity represents an important element of a holy life, so diligently avoid behavior that leads to sexual iniquity.

Third, grace looks to "the blessed hope and glorious appearing of our great God and Savior Jesus Christ" (Titus 2:13). Anyone who sincerely accepts God's grace earnestly looks for the day of His return. He adopts a focus that prepares him for appearing in the presence of the Lord. A firm belief that Jesus is coming again motivates the believer to assume an eternal perspective in living this life. He recognizes that relationships matter far more than possessions, and bearing fruit for God is of more value than building a comfortable life. In anticipation of His return, he meditates on His character and holiness, to become more like Him. Moreover, he cultivates a passion for identifying where and how God is at work in his neighborhood, country, and across the world and investigates how to join Him in each of those areas. That passion evidences itself in his prioritization of time. For example, he may determine to invest a few vacation days or even a couple weeks doing God's work in some capacity, such as a short-term mission assignment, volunteering at a local pregnancy center, or helping refugees get settled in his community. While this diverts some vacation time away from his enjoyment, grace teaches him to value sharing God's love more than a comfortable vacation because grace looks to the "glorious appearing of our great God and Savior Jesus Christ."

Fourth, grace bestows upon us the privilege to call Him Lord and spend eternity with Him, and represents the means God uses to restore people into relationship with Him. His sacrifice "redeems us from every lawless deed and purifies for Himself His own people" (Titus 2:14). God's grace redeems us from our sinful past, through the shed blood of Jesus. No matter how wicked our behavior or how sinful an act we committed, we are redeemed. Jesus atones for all our past and future iniquities. However, His sacrifice does this for a specific purpose—to purify us for Himself. He desires a relationship with each one of us and, more importantly, He desires a relationship with *you*. But our sin precludes fellowship with God because He will not permit sin in His presence. So our sin must be atoned for through the shedding of blood (Hebrews 9:22), which Jesus accomplishes through His crucified death. In this redemptive act, Jesus purifies us so we are able to fellowship with the Father. Knowing that, why would any Christian return to his sinful conduct or pursue again any lifestyle of sin? He wouldn't if a genuine believer for he knows he belongs to God's "own people."

Fifth, grace makes us "zealous for good works" (Titus 2:14). We develop a zeal for committing good works. We desire to serve others and leave a spiritual impact on those around us. We establish a pattern of behavior and service that meets the needs of those in our local community as well as those halfway around the world. Why? We realize God extended mercy to us when we were lost and had no hope of salvation. A clear comprehension of the magnitude of His gift excites us to a life of service and good works. We respond with unmitigated joy at being His ambassador in the world and demonstrating love and mercy to others as a fractional example of what He extended to us. We desire others experience grace, so we conduct ourselves with an eye toward committing good works that we might draw people to Him. Where grace truly exists, good works occur. Keep in mind we do not perform these works for our credit, to receive approval from others, or burnish our reputation. They are a product of grace and we glorify Christ for the opportunity to complete them.

Paul captures the essence of these truths more succinctly in his epistle to the church at Corinth when he tells them, "Therefore, if anyone is in Christ, he is a new creation; old things have passed away, behold all things have become new" (2 Corinthians 5:17). Paul does not mince words about the possibility or likelihood of a believer undergoing a complete transformation. He instructs us that every believer is a new creation *if* he is in Christ. No one who sincerely submits to Jesus as Lord retains his prior lifestyle. He does not continue in ungodliness or the pursuit of worldly lusts, but seeks righteousness in expectation of the Lord, who purified him for fellowship with the Father and to commit good works. Otherwise, his behavior demonstrates an insincere commitment to God.

Do not allow Satan to persuade you that such significant change is optional. He has used that lie to convince multitudes of Americans, including many within the church, that grace provides salvation but has no other purpose in the life of a believer. He has persuaded many that grace does not require change, since God created us to behave the way we do. That is a lie he has used for centuries—even selling that argument to the Israelites thousands of years ago. Through Jeremiah, God informed the nation of Judah, "Behold, you trust in lying words that cannot profit. Will you steal, murder, commit adultery, swear falsely, burn incense to Baal, and walk after other gods whom you do not know, and then come and stand before Me in this house which is called by My name, and say, 'We are delivered to do all these abominations'" (Jeremiah 7:8-10). The Israelites believed they could live in sin while claiming to be God's people, that a worldly lifestyle was compatible with faith. In fact, they had the temerity to declare that God had delivered them to commit iniquity. They actually argued that the grace of God freed them from their enemies for the purpose of living in wickedness. What a distorted view; the Israelites failed to understand that God is holy and hates sin. Not surprisingly, they suffered God's judgment. We need to learn this important lesson from the Israelites—the grace of Jesus yields holiness not continued sin. God's grace is not a license to pursue worldly lusts. If we follow the Israelites' pattern, God will tell us the same thing He told them, "You trust in lying words that cannot profit."

Does your life evidence the behavior grace teaches? Have you ceased the ungodly conduct and worldly lusts that enveloped your life before you encountered Jesus? Do you live a more righteous and holy life as a member of God's family? Has your focus become eternal-oriented as a believer? Does your life exhibit good works done for God's glory? If a candid examination of your life reveals little progress in these areas, it is possible you never really accepted God's grace. Your faith may reflect an intellectual exercise or be grounded in a selfish desire to avoid hell. If so, seek out the Holy Spirit and ask Him to reveal the true condition of your heart and a deep appreciation for what grace represents. Your life will never be the same.

QUESTIONS:

1. We often learn that grace restores our fellowship with God. According to Paul's counsel to Titus, what else does it do?

2. Why does grace call us to live godly and righteously?

3. God's redemption purifies the believer. What benefit does this produce for the believer?

Who through faith subdued kingdoms, worked righteousness, obtained promises, stopped the mouths of lions, quenched the violence of fire, escaped the edge of the sword, out of weakness were made strong, became valiant in battle, turned to flight the armies of the aliens. Women received their dead raised to life again.

—Hebrews 11:33-35

CHAPTER 6

Cost of Discipleship

Many believe their faith automatically leads to immense exploits like those described in Hebrews because our Christian leaders often teach it as an immutable truth. They provide an example or two from Scripture as evidence all believers should expect such outcomes. They suggest God wants His people to enjoy considerable success in life. He works in His saint's lives so they accomplish great things in their jobs resulting in significant career success. He magnifies their opportunities at work and helps them achieve a higher level of performance so they realize their dreams. While some pastors and leaders teach a more subtle version, the teaching's basic tenet is that God desires this result for all who trust Him. The Bible, however, recounts example after example of God's people who suffer unimaginable harm and difficulty because they possessed authentic faith and acted on it. So how do we reconcile these two perspectives, and how does the passage in Hebrews inform us about God's plan for believers?

Recall that Hebrews 11 provides a fascinating "highlight reel" of those who followed and obeyed God in the Old Testament and how their faithfulness impacted their lives. It describes many of the great icons of faith from the Old Testament, the paragons of authentic faith. They represent what it means to live by faith and what we can expect if we live by faith as well. After spending much of the chapter describing the lives of several specific people of faith, the author notes that many more examples of faith exist that he could have shared as well. He then describes the exploits that those of faith have performed: "Who through faith subdued kingdoms, worked righteousness, obtained promises, stopped the mouths of lions, quenched the violence of fire, escaped the edge of the sword, out of weakness were made strong, became valiant in battle, turned to flight the armies of the aliens. Women received their dead raised to life again" (Hebrews 11:33-35).

Those verses describe a faith that most would agree sounds really exciting. After all, who doesn't want to subdue kingdoms, cause entire armies to retreat, or raise the dead to life? Those achievements are really awesome! If such exploits represent what people of faith will accomplish, then "count me in," we say. Those are the types of success we want to achieve and the outcomes we want our faith to deliver, or at least the modern equivalent for the twenty-first century.

Unfortunately, too many pastors and teachers emphasize this and similar Scripture, telling us this path does indeed represent what God wants for us. But they read these verses in isolation and never in the context of the broader themes of discipleship Jesus preached. They avoid passages demonstrating those most faithful to God were more likely to experience difficult lives than comfortable ones. Their success was evidenced by obedience, not wealth or career achievements. But instead we learn from too many leaders that the Lord strengthens His disciples so they overcome whatever difficulties they face and experience success in their lives and their careers. They might suggest the following represent modern versions of how God wants His faithful to succeed.

- Lead businesses successfully.
- Cause competitors to retreat.
- Demonstrate strong leadership at work.
- Bring dying patients back to life.
- Escape economic downturns.
- Quench the challenges that keep us from success.
- Act valiantly in our jobs.
- Receive promises.

Many Christian leaders use these Old Testament examples to reinforce the message that lots of believers want to hear; they represent what congregants have come to expect for followers of Jesus. We expect this level of success at work and in our careers. We have accepted the perspective that believers experience career success and do great things in our professions. While only the most brazen teachers assert something like, "If you love Jesus, you will enjoy tremendous success", much of the American church teaches a similar message, in slightly less candid language. They 'hint' and 'imply' God wants His people to have rewarding careers, regular promotions, prestigious positions, and deliver impressive results.

But nothing in Scripture supports any of this. We believe this perspective is biblical either because we have heard it over and over, or because we *want* to believe it. We want such outcomes from our faith. We want God infinitely concerned with our career success. We want God desperate to make us great leaders in the corporate, legal, medical, educational, and media industries. We desire a God who yearns to bless us with exciting, fulfilling jobs that yield incredible economic benefit.

How poorly we understand the Bible if we believe God's desire is to heap success on us in the careers we choose. God's desire for us is that we redeem our time here on earth for His glory and to advance His kingdom until He returns (or calls us home). He focuses on the impact our careers have on others and how we use our position to bring Him glory, not on whether we get a prestigious promotion or plumb new assignment.

Now it is possible that as we seek to honor Him at work, we may advance in whatever field we pursue. However, as with Esther, it is only so He can then use us to take a stand for Him; that we use our position to influence others as He guides us and provides us an opportunity. (See Esther 4-8). It is never for our own glory or worldly benefit.

If God does provide you an especially successful career, it is because He has a plan to use that for His glory. Very likely He wants you to regularly share your faith with colleagues at work and others in your field. He wants you to set an example with the highest level of integrity, which may negatively impact your career advancement when you do not compromise. He wants you to speak up for righteousness and godliness in how your company conducts its business and not follow the world's approach that emphasizes profit. If you do not possess the boldness of faith to confront your company when it operates in a manner against God's principles, then God will probably not put you in a leadership position. (For several examples of boldness in sharing truth with resistant leaders, see 1 Kings 18:17-18 and 1 Kings 22:1-28).

The remainder of Hebrews 11 is absolutely critical to understand fully God's plan. He is as likely to call you to a life of difficulty and challenge as He is to a life of success, perhaps more so. In fact, only the most spiritually mature are likely called to the latter since it presents considerable temptation to compromise faith and often leads to an idolatrous love for the world. But we need to understand the real possibility that our faith leads to an uncomfortable and challenging life, especially in America where we tend to avoid difficulty with every fiber of our being.

The remainder of Hebrews 11 explains what other faithful followers of God experienced. "And others were tortured, not accepting deliverance, that they might obtain a better resurrection. Still others had trial of mockings and scourging, yes, and of chains and imprisonment. They were stoned, they were sawn in two, were tempted, were slain with the sword. They wandered about in sheepskins and goatskins, being destitute, afflicted, tormented—of whom the world was not worthy. They wandered in deserts and mountains, in dens and caves of the earth" (Hebrews 11:35-38).

Wow!

Take a minute to reread that passage, slowly. Focus on what godly men of faith faced in the Old Testament. This passage reflects a powerful contrast to the section we read earlier. Surprisingly, both sections reflect the accomplishments of those who live by faith. But who wants any of the exploits described in these latter verses?

Who wants to be tortured?

Anyone desire to be mocked or imprisoned for his or her faith?

Who wants to suffer physical violence for believing in God?

Any volunteers to be forced on the run or in hiding, or live destitute lives due to their faith?

In the United States we generally ignore the second half of the passage. "Not sure how that got in there," we might tell ourselves. "My God would *never* want *me* to live that kind of life. He wants me living like a king, not a pauper," we may proclaim. What arrogance we demonstrate in uttering such views. God's Word asserts this is exactly the kind of life we may face if we live boldly for Him with a selfless and sacrificial faith. We should recognize such a life is a real possibility.

Our typical response to this passage characterizes how "me-focused" our faith has become. We do not believe God wants twenty-first-century American Christians subjected to the same consequences of faith that all our predecessors were subjected. Only a faith grounded in unbridled selfishness, pride, and superiority would presume God willingly subjected many believers to such lives across the centuries and across all geographies today, but that He has a better plan for American Christians, that He chooses us alone to bless with successful careers and comfortable lives.

Alternatively, we explain away the second half of the passage by asserting our willingness to suffer such treatment for Jesus if necessary, but since we live in a country with religious freedom we are not subjected to such suffering. There are two issues with that perspective. First, if we truly live boldly for Christ we will definitely suffer the mockings and contempt of others (we explore this in detail in chapter 25). We may not suffer death, but we will definitely put our careers and success at risk. We do not suffer because we are too timid in our faith, at work and in our community. We do not want to appear too radical. We want to avoid others perceiving us as overly religious. So we frequently temper our faith around others. Second, the passage is about the exploits of those who have faith. If you possess genuine faith, you need to consider that God may call you to a life where you are subjected to such outcomes.

Perhaps God is calling you as a missionary.

Maybe He is calling you to take a stand for righteousness at work.

Possibly He wants you bolder about your faith with your social club or your neighbors.

Likely He is calling you to live a faith more observable to the world around you.

Almost certainly He wants you offering a contrast to the way the world lives, by living and speaking the standards He has established.

It is even possible He is calling you to resign from your corporate or professional job and pursue a "career" serving Him in some capacity (at a much lower income but higher satisfaction).

Yes, obedience to such callings could negatively impact your reputation, success, status, and even your career if word gets out that you (shhh!) love Jesus. But as with Esther, you must realize that God puts you in situations for His purpose. If you disobey, He will accomplish His plan through someone else and you will go unused. (See Esther 4:13-14). The expectation of a challenging and difficult life for those who follow God is not limited to Old Testament figures. Jesus communicated the same message during His ministry.

"Now it happened as they journeyed on the road, that someone said to Him, 'Lord, I will follow You wherever You go.' And Jesus said to him, 'Foxes have holes and birds of the air have nests, but the Son of Man has nowhere to lay His head.' Then He said to another, 'Follow Me.' But he said, 'Lord, let me first go and bury my father.' Jesus said to him, 'Let the dead bury their own dead, but you go and preach the kingdom of God.' And another also said, 'Lord, I will follow You, but let me first go and bid them farewell who are at my house.' But Jesus said to him, 'No one, having put his hand to the plow, and looking back, is fit for the kingdom of God'" (Luke 9:57-62).

Jesus uses these three examples to communicate several vital truths about discipleship. First, following Him will be difficult and often uncomfortable. He told the first responder that He had no home but lived the life of an itinerant prophet. While God certainly does not call everyone to that lifestyle, He does call every one of us to live sacrificially. Often He will command us down a path that runs counter to the lifestyle of comfort to which we are accustomed. He wants to know whether we truly trust Him as Lord and will obey Him no matter the cost, or whether our obedience and commitment only extends as far as our flesh and selfishness allows.

Second, He wants to take precedence over other commitments and interests. The second responder affirmed a willingness to follow Jesus but only after he tended to another commitment, the burying of his dad. Jesus' response reminds us that the cost of discipleship requires we set aside our own interests, however reasonable and valid they seem to the world. He has called us to obey and pursue the Great Commission, and we must avoid competing or distracting priorities.

Third, following Jesus means we must count all things as loss, even relationships we value. This does not mean we end all relationships; it simply indicates that those relationships must be secondary to our obedience and commitment to the Lord. Too often we believe Jesus adjusts His will for us so it does not disrupt our relationships with friends and family. We think that whenever the needs or expectations of a loved one conflicts with God's plan, then God will change His plan accordingly. Jesus clearly rebukes that perspective in the three examples He shared. Such difficult truths prevent many from following the Lord, but even Jesus experienced the departure of many disciples once they learned how difficult the path was in following Christ (see John 6:65-66).

The author of Hebrews identifies Old Testament prophets and people who lived the faithful life Jesus emphasized. They demonstrated the selflessness, humility, and commitment Jesus calls each of His disciples to follow, and showed a willingness to suffer and bear all manner of difficulty as a result. They did this by setting aside their own desires and following God's will no matter the cost. Jesus told us we should adopt the same approach and expect similar outcomes as we follow and obey Him. It certainly results in a much different lifestyle than what our flesh desires. Nevertheless, we can embrace the difficulty He sends our way knowing it brings Him glory and represents obedience.

1. Many Americans believe Christians in other countries suffer because they live in pagan countries while we do not suffer because ours is Christian. Do you see any flaws with that view?

2. Hebrews recounts numerous examples of Old Testament figures who lived difficult lives due to their faith. Jesus indicates that anyone who follows Him will also face difficulty. In what ways has your life been difficult as a direct result of your faith? In what ways is the Lord calling you to a more difficult life?

3. Why is it hard to believe a faithful life often leads to a more challenging and difficult life? Why does God often make life challenging for believers? What benefit do we derive from such a life?

But what things were gain to me, these I have counted loss for Christ. But indeed I count all things loss for the excellence of the knowledge of Christ Jesus my Lord, for whom I have suffered the loss of all things, and count them as rubbish, that I might gain Christ and be found in Him, not having my own righteousness which is from the law, but that which is through faith in Christ, the righteousness which is from God by faith.; that I may know Him and the power of His resurrection, and the fellowship of His sufferings being conformed to His death.

—Philippians 3:7-10

CHAPTER 7

Count All as Loss

Paul captures the perspective held by those who have genuine faith in Jesus. He notes that "what things were gain to me, these I have counted loss for Christ." Prior to coming to faith in Jesus, Paul had many things working to his advantage including his reputation, his status as a Jew and Pharisee, his status of appearing blameless by the law, and his position as a leader in the community. No doubt these advantages provided him a nice income and a comfortable lifestyle. He enjoyed a great career and was well positioned for future success throughout life. Figuratively speaking, he was on top of the world. Yet on coming to Christ, Paul counts *all* those things as loss. Maintaining any of them would require him to compromise his new faith. He could not retain his reputation once he boldly proclaimed Jesus as Lord. Remaining a Pharisee was impossible once he explicitly embraced the Teacher who had openly condemned the Pharisees for their hypocrisy. Continuing as a leader who persecuted the church was out of the question once he joined the church.

So he counted as loss all those benefits he previously enjoyed. He dismissed them. No longer would his life reflect those advantages. In the process, of course, he would lose the ancillary benefits that came with those things. His income would disappear. His reputation would fall from sterling to scoundrel. He would lose his friends. He would lose his power. He would lose his status. He would lose his influence. But he willingly gave all of that up for Christ. He knew having an authentic relationship with Jesus required significant change, and that change would never occur if he tried to live with one foot in his old world and one foot in the new.

So he counted the cost of becoming a disciple of Jesus. It was an easy decision once he laid out the equation. He gave up all the incredible benefits and advantages of being an esteemed Jewish leader and Pharisee and replaced that with the life of an itinerant preacher. While his quality of life took a nosedive from the perspective of the nonbeliever, Paul looked to the promise of eternity. Trading a couple dozen years of the good life on earth in exchange for an eternity with the living God was a no-brainer.

What about you? Have you counted all things as loss for Christ? In what areas of your pre-Christian life do you maintain a grip? In what areas of gain have you failed to count as loss for Jesus? Do you continue to burnish your reputation, but at the expense of being a bold witness for Jesus? Do you pursue your career with such zeal that your Christian witness never materializes? Do you have friends with whom you would be embarrassed to share the gospel and how Jesus is your Lord, so they remain unaware of your faith? Do you fervently protect your status with your peers and neighbors, even if that means using foul language, watching inappropriate videos, gossiping, and drinking in excess? Do you adopt a worldly disposition when you go "out with the guys" or have a girls' weekend, in order to remain "cool" and "in the clique"?

It is a tremendous temptation to deny or ignore our faith in any area we continue to harbor as "gain." If those areas remain important to us, we easily succumb to temptation and compromise our faith in order to maintain the gain. That is why Paul explained we must count all those things as loss. Give up on them entirely. Cast off the burden of maintaining a reputation. Cease to prioritize your career. Dismiss the desire to be cool and popular. Determine to hold no status with any group or friends. Once you count all those things as loss, you will no longer spend time trying to retain them. You will no longer feel enticement to compromise your faith over them.

Paul declares that he does not simply count as loss those things that were previously "gain" to him but counts "*all* things loss for the excellence of the knowledge of Christ Jesus my Lord, for whom I have suffered the loss of *all* things, and count them as *rubbish*, that I may gain Christ." He goes even further and says he will count everything in this world as loss and count it all as if it were garbage. He counts his lifestyle as trash. He counts his success as worthless. He counts his popularity and reputation as nothing. He counts his comfort and safety as useless. He counts it *all* as loss. Why? That he might know Christ more intimately and spend more time with Him. That was the one thing Paul desired above all else: to know Jesus. To develop as much as possible his relationship with Jesus, Paul decided to count everything in his life as loss. That would minimize any distractions that interfered with knowing His Lord more and more.

What about you? What things in life distract you from developing a closer relationship with Jesus? What interferes with you knowing the Lord more intimately each day? Are you prepared to count those things as loss? Will you join Paul in counting them as rubbish that you might become more familiar with Jesus and His character?

Until he counts all things as rubbish, Paul knows he will face daily temptation to pursue them. He will invest considerable time and effort in anything he values in this world. So he determines to count it all as worthless, not worth making any effort to pursue. As a result, he frees up considerable time and energy to focus on knowing the Lord more closely and developing a deeper relationship with Him. Does that seem radical? Well, it is radical. But it represents the view we need to adopt as believers.

Sadly, many of our lives reflect a desire to be entertained, pleasured, and comforted instead. That stands in stark contrast to what Paul says about his effort to count all things as loss "for the excellence of the knowledge of Christ Jesus my Lord." Is Jesus really your Lord? If so, what are you doing to know Him more intimately? How serious are you about developing a closer relationship with Him? Do you make every effort to spend as much of your free time with Him as possible, or are you more focused on spending time with friends, watching sports, shopping for clothes, exercising, reading novels, and other activities that do nothing to draw you closer to Jesus?

Unfortunately, most of us devote little time to knowing Christ more dearly. Our actions reveal how little we value that aspiration, often viewing it as a grudging obligation rather than a pursuit of excellence as Paul did. We look to squeeze in ten or fifteen minutes here and there, but we dedicate the bulk of our free time to pursuing our own interests and satisfying our own passions. We count very little as loss in order to know Jesus more personally. In fact, many of us count nothing as loss for the excellence of knowing Christ more deeply. As a result, our faith offers little power to impact the world for Jesus. Worse, it may reveal an artificial faith that looks good on the outside but on the inside lacks authenticity.

So what are the benefits of counting all things as loss that you might know Christ more closely? Paul indicates several:

- You have the righteousness of Jesus. This is different than the righteousness from the law, which no one can achieve since all far short. It is an imputed righteousness granted to all who place their faith in Jesus and submit to Him as Lord. It is the righteousness that leads to salvation.
- You have the power of His resurrection. The Holy Spirit sits on those who make an earnest profession of faith in Jesus and who demonstrate this faith by counting all things as loss for His glory. That power manifested itself through the apostles in the early church, which lead thousands to a saving knowledge of the Lord across the Mediterranean (see Acts 2:47).
- We participate in His suffering. We learn to obey Him in all things no matter how it impacts our life, even unto death. We learn to value His glory as more precious and important than our own well-being, health and safety. This makes us far more useful for accomplishing His will on Earth.

All this equates to knowing Jesus more closely, His attributes more fully, and identifying His will more clearly. It equates to knowing His power more substantively and His grace more effectively.

Having counted all things as loss for Christ, what impact did Paul's decision have on his life? He tells the church at Corinth, "To the present hour we both hunger and thirst, and we are poorly clothed, and beaten, and homeless. And we labor, working with our own hands. Being reviled, we bless; being persecuted, we endure it; being defamed, we entreat. We have been made as the filth of the world, the offscouring of all things until now" (1 Corinthians 4:11-13). Paul describes how his life bore considerable suffering. Before becoming a disciple of Jesus, Paul enjoyed a life of wealth, status, influence, power, and comfort. After counting the cost to follow Christ, he experienced poverty, persecution, and pain while suffering the reviling, defamation, and contempt of the world. How could someone who had so many advantages in life embrace with joy a new life with such difficulty and hurt? Paul was able because he knew the Lord intimately and had counted the cost of discipleship when he became a Christian.

Too many of us make professions of faith without really understanding our commitment or without counting the cost. We never consider how following Jesus will impact our lifestyle and priorities, or inquire about the expectations Jesus has for us if we make Him Lord. As a result, we express surprise to learn that following Jesus costs everything (read Luke14:25-33, where Jesus describes the considerable challenge of being His disciple and asserts, "So, likewise, whoever of you does not forsake all that he has cannot be My disciple."). Following Jesus is no walk in the park, and does not come without a cost—indeed, quite a serious cost.

Until one counts the cost of becoming a disciple, he cannot expect to fully obey Jesus. He will not lay down his own advantages for the glory of God because he does not believe he must. He does not count all things as loss, indeed as rubbish, for the excellence of knowing Christ because his sin nature resists. Have you learned to count all things in your life as loss that you might know Jesus more substantively and develop a deeper relationship with Him?

QUESTIONS:

1. Identify an area or two in your life that you have refrained from counting as loss for Christ. Why do you seek to retain control in this area?

2. What specific steps will you take to count these areas as loss for Jesus moving forward?

3. Why is it so critical that we count *all* things as loss and even view them as rubbish in our lives?

Again, the kingdom of heaven is like treasure hidden in a field, which a man found and hid; and for joy over it he goes and sells all that he has and buys that field.

—Matthew 13:44

CHAPTER 8

Salvation Costs Everything

In this story a man happens upon hidden treasure, a metaphor for the kingdom of heaven. Jesus does not indicate whether he was looking for it. However, upon discovering it he immediately recognizes its value. He understands the blessing this treasure represents. How does he respond to finding the treasure? Jesus tells His disciples the man is overjoyed. He cannot believe his good fortune. He recognizes there existed little likelihood of just stumbling upon such immeasurable treasure. He realizes he must not allow an opportunity of this magnitude to get away.

Getting that treasure, though, will cost him *everything*. He does not negotiate with the property owner to secure a lower price because he does not want to risk losing the opportunity to buy the field and obtain the treasure. If he pursues negotiation, the owner may decide he is being stingy and revoke the sale offer; or maybe someone else steps in during the negotiation process and buys the property for more than he can afford. The man knows that if he really wants this treasure, he must go all-in and invest everything he has to acquire the property.

But you know what he did when confronted with the reality that this treasure would cost him everything? He sold all he had and did so joyfully. He did not behave begrudgingly, frustrated that the treasure had such an extreme cost. He did not say to himself, "I can't believe this landowner is going to make me sell everything to buy his field containing hidden treasure." On the contrary, he was ecstatic! He willingly and enthusiastically sold everything he owned. His unbridled joy derived from the fact that he focused on the benefit of possessing the treasure rather than turning his attention on the cost. Although the cost accounted for everything he had, the benefit far outweighed it. Did that mean it was an easy proposition? Of course not. It was difficult. No doubt he was attached to many of the possessions he had to sell. But with the proper focus and an understanding of true value, the man made the best decision.

Observe the haste with which the man acts. He goes into action immediately. He does not ruminate over his options or seek counsel from friends or his investment advisor. His decision requires no calculator. He does not need an appraisal for his possessions. He instantly comprehends the disparity in value between the two options and acts quickly, for time is of the essence.

We learn three important lessons about the man obtaining the kingdom of heaven:

1. It costs him everything.
2. He responds with joy.
3. He acts immediately.

Too often we respond much differently in our faith. We read that verse in the context of our twenty-first-century American lifestyle and convince ourselves that the man's response was not literal. Jesus did not mean the man gave up everything to get the land. We reject the notion that a believer must give up anything to acquire the kingdom of heaven. We tell ourselves salvation reflects a gift from God and therefore costs us nothing. We cling to this belief because it aligns with our sin nature. While we rightly understand God's grace saves us, we fail to understand it costs us everything.

Unfortunately, many pastors and believers ignore the hard truth of this parable and explain away the message Jesus delivers. They argue that because we cannot earn salvation on the front-end, God does not require anything on the back-end as an output of our faith. Grace provides salvation for free on the front-end and mercy covers our subsequent sin on the back-end after we believe. We learn that the gift of eternal life and its benefits do not require anything from us. Essentially, we learn that we do not pay anything for the field. In the modern American version of this parable, the landowner invites the stranger onto his property and simply gives him the treasure for free. Nothing required and no strings attached. It is the gift of the landowner because he desires the stranger's happiness and contentment. But that viewpoint contradicts what Jesus actually said.

Jesus' message clearly taught that a cost existed; the man who wanted the kingdom of heaven gives up everything to receive it. Obviously, Jesus is not implying we purchase salvation with currency. Instead, He indicates we must give up everything upon salvation—not to earn it but in response to receiving it. Take a minute to consider what constitutes everything. Jesus provides no exceptions for what the man gave up to secure heaven. Essentially, everything means *every thing*. More than just our possessions, it requires we give up non-material things as well.

- Dreams.
- Careers.
- Reputation.
- Popularity.
- Relationships.
- Free time.
- Discretionary income.
- Lifestyle.

In coming to faith in Jesus we must give up everything we hold dear. We must set aside all that we value so those things do not distract us from following the Lord. We do all this for joy! Recognizing the blessing of salvation that Jesus' blood purchased for us, we gladly give up all to follow Him. This does not represent a burden to bear but a labor of love. Is it difficult to give up everything? Absolutely. Our flesh relentlessly fights us, making all manner of excuses for why we should not give up everything for Jesus. "That is a works-based faith" our sinful heart tells us. "Jesus wants us happy" our spirit of selfishness informs us. But no excuse holds up against the truth of Scripture, and Jesus tells us unambiguously that the path of faith costs everything.

Acts captures an example of this from the early church. Following an incident in which a multitude witnessed the power of God, we learn that "the name of the Lord Jesus was magnified. And many who had believed came confessing and telling their deeds. Also, many of those who had practiced magic brought their books together and burned them in the sight of all. And they counted up the value of them, and it totaled fifty thousand pieces of silver. So the word of the Lord grew mightily and prevailed" (Acts 19:17-20).

Notice that those who believed confessed their sins before the people. They made a public profession of faith. But they did not continue to live a lifestyle of sin after verbalizing faith in Jesus. Those who practiced magic burned the books they used in their craft, and apparently the cost was considerable. These new believers did not attempt to graft their new faith into their old lifestyle. They did not seek a hybrid faith that allowed them to confess Christ as Savior while continuing to pursue worldly activities. They understood that genuine faith requires leaving the old life behind and becoming new in Jesus. They had learned the importance of giving up everything for God and were able to walk away from a livelihood that dishonored Him.

Hebrews provides another powerful example of someone who gave up everything for faith. In writing about Moses, the author declares, "By faith Moses, when he became of age, refused to be called the son of Pharaoh's daughter, choosing rather to suffer affliction with the people of God than to enjoy the passing pleasures of sin, esteeming the reproach of Christ greater riches than the treasures in Egypt; for he looked to the reward. By faith he forsook Egypt, not fearing the wrath of the king; for he endured as seeing Him who is invisible" (Hebrews 11:24-27). Moses' faith spurred him to action. He made decisions demonstrating his commitment to God rather than fulfilling the desires of his flesh. He could have remained in Pharaoh's mansion and enjoyed all the comfort, luxury, and extravagance to which he was entitled as Pharaoh's grandson. He could have told himself that such a lifestyle reflected God's blessing and was a result of his faith. I suspect a great many of us would have taken this approach because we often tell ourselves something similar today.

But Moses held a decidedly different view. He refused to exercise his rights as the son of Pharaoh's daughter. When he surveyed all the benefits of being a part of Pharaoh's family, he did not see blessing, he saw sin. Staying in the mansion and living a life of luxury and comfort appealed to his flesh, but did not appeal to his spirit. Such a life focused on self rather than others; it worshipped Moses, not God. So he rejected that path. He recognized it represented his sin nature. Rather than demonstrate his faith, pursuing that selfish course of action would actually diminish his faith. It would not reveal God's favor but rather remove God's favor as he chose selfishness over obedience.

So Moses chose to suffer affliction with his Hebrew brethren. He left the lifestyle to which he was accustomed and to which he was entitled and lived a considerably more difficult life with his fellow followers of God. Can you imagine making that decision? Leaving a lifestyle that all the world views as the pinnacle of success and which offers every imaginable comfort; where servants exist solely to meet your needs and desires. But Moses chose a life of hard labor instead, working long days in the sun. Rather than living in the comfort of the mansion, Moses chose to build the bricks that were used to make the mansion. He made the decision because he esteemed "the reproach of Christ greater riches than the treasures in Egypt." He viewed an unbearably difficult life with Christ of far more value than a life enjoying the vast wealth of Egypt.

He held such a view because he knew God. He had an intimate relationship with Him and knew that obeying the Lord was more important than satisfying his sin nature. He "looked to the reward" that would come when he arrived in heaven. Hearing God tell him, "Well done, my good and faithful servant" was of much greater value than experiencing every pleasure and comfort of this world. Serving

God had eternal value, so he obeyed. He understood that sincere faith sacrifices.

We read how Moses responded and might think he was foolish. Why not remain in Pharaoh's house *and* live for God. We convince ourselves that a hybrid approach represents the best response. But Moses understood that the two were incompatible with one another. He could not obey the Lord if He remained beholden to the cares of this world living in the mansion. Moreover, he refused to live a life of comfort and pleasure while his brethren suffered and labored in the fields. He recognized that would reflect a heart of incredible arrogance and selfishness.

We, too, have brethren who labor and suffer in the fields today. They work relentlessly to harvest the fields of souls God is calling to Himself. Across the world our brothers and sisters in the Lord labor tirelessly to fulfill the Great Commission. Their obedience often leads to suffering and their efforts frequently meet with resistance and rejection. But they persevere because, like Moses, they esteem the reproach of this world of no consequence in comparison to the love of Christ. Meanwhile, we often remain in Pharaoh's mansion telling ourselves that God calls us to a life of luxury and ease.

QUESTIONS:

1. How does your sinful nature want you to respond to the verses we examined in Matthew and Hebrews? Are you living in Pharaoh's mansion? If so, what lesson might you learn from Moses?

2. What areas of life have you yet to yield to Jesus? Why are you waiting?

3. Do you live sacrificially for the Lord? Do you do so for joy or begrudgingly? What keeps you from responding with joy?

PART III

Difficult because:
We Must Not Love the World

The American church has had a profoundly positive impact on the world since the founding of this nation. From sending a multitude of missionaries to Asia, Africa, and Latin America and establishing the faith in many countries there, to raising up preachers God used to convert untold millions to Christianity, to tremendous works of human compassion for people in need, the American church likely has had no equal in its influence and effect on the world. It is sad, then, to observe a national church so instrumental in advancing the kingdom of God and submitting to the Lord's leadership in fulfilling His plan the past two hundred fifty-plus years now begin to sink into irrelevance. But such is the course the American church has charted for itself as it pursues a path of compromise with the world. As a result, God is using more than ever other nations and peoples to fulfill His Great Commission while the American church chases other passions and priorities.

What caused this incomprehensible decline in the power of the American church? Why has she become far less relevant in bringing the good news of Jesus to her countrymen in the United States as well as to the unsaved across the world? What led to her diminished influence in positively impacting the country and the world for the glory of God?

I firmly believe her increased love for the world has crippled her effectiveness for the Lord. The church has fallen so in love with the things of this world and all it offers that she no longer prioritizes her relationship with God first. Consequently, her focus has shifted from the Lord and His will to the world and its pleasures. The result has been disastrous. What started as a flirtatious relationship with the world has become a full-fledged affair. The church's passion for and allegiance to the world has taken on an idolatrous nature. She wants to blend her declining commitment to the Lord with her burgeoning obsession for the things of the world. That puts her squarely in the crosshairs of God's judgment. He has been patient, waiting for us to repent. At some point, though, He will no longer tolerate our idolatry with the world and we will face His judgment.

The next seven chapters explore how the American church pursues this adulterous affair with the world and how we demonstrate our passionate love for it. We examine Scripture that warns of the serious danger awaiting those who become involved with the world. We consider the consequences facing anyone prioritizing the things of this world above the things of God. We discuss what the church must do with immediacy if she hopes to return to her first love and avoid judgment. It will be extremely difficult because our love for the world is so deep and so integrated into our faith. But Jesus said the path that leads to life would be difficult, so we must identify this sin, repent, reject the world, and return to the Lord. There is still time, but very little.

May the Holy Spirit give each believer wisdom to understand His truth in each passage we investigate and convict us so we immediately stop this adulterous affair and renew with vigor our relationship with Jesus Christ.

Then one from the crowd said to Him, "Teacher, tell my brother to divide the inheritance with me." But He said to him, "Man, who made me a judge or an arbitrator over you?" And He said to them, "Take heed and beware of covetousness, for one's life does not consist in the abundance of the things he possesses." Then He spoke a parable to them, saying: "The ground of a certain rich man yielded plentifully. And he thought within himself, saying 'What shall I do, since I have no room to store my crops?' So he said, 'I will do this: I will pull down my barns and build greater, and there I will store all my crops and my goods. And I will say to my soul, "Soul, you have many goods laid up for many years; take your ease; eat, drink, and be merry."' But God said to him, "You fool! This night your soul will be required of you; then whose will those things be which you have provided?"

So is he who lays up treasure for himself, and is not rich toward God.

—Luke 12:13-21

CHAPTER 9

The Good Life

Our society celebrates the American dream, which increasingly means living "the good life." Enjoying the latest technology, the newest "toys," and a lifestyle of comfort, leisure, and entertainment reflect this. We fund this life through hard work climbing up the corporate ladder in a chosen profession in which increased success yields increased income. In the American dream the individual is held in high esteem. Our culture celebrates the individual who pulls himself up by his bootstraps and accomplishes much through his own ingenuity, diligence, and perseverance. Society instructs us that whatever benefits and wealth result from such efforts are entirely the individuals' to enjoy. "You earned it," society proclaims, and therefore entitled to enjoy the spoils.

But "the good life" does not comport with what Jesus taught His followers; such a lifestyle is inconsistent with discipleship. Many of us embrace "the good life" message because of the lifestyle it offers and its recognition of the importance of self, despite Jesus' reproach against that view. Many Christians want to live the "good life" and remain followers of Jesus. We want the life of comfort, pleasure, and leisure enjoyed by our secular friends yet claim fellowship with the Lord. But Jesus warned against this temptation. He understood that many of His followers would remain in love with the world while claiming to confess Him as Lord. Knowing the appeal this temptation would have, He emphasized its illegitimacy. His admonition erased any doubt around the compatibility between sincere faith and living the good life.

Unfortunately, too many of us have dismissed this warning as irrelevant, assuming it applies to others. That is a surprising response since the warning seems custom tailored for the American church. In fact, the parable of the wealthy farmer at the beginning of the chapter should convict us to the heart. Do you immediately relate to this rich fool, saying to yourself something like, "Wow, he sounds a lot like me. I also exhibit a heart of covetousness and a selfish attitude." If so, take some time to seek God's forgiveness and ask Him to effect the requisite change in your heart. If not, ask the Holy Spirit to reveal biblical truth to you as you read through the chapter; pray that He makes known any covetousness that exists in your spirit.

The vast majority of Christians typically respond to this passage in one of the following manners, or a combination thereof:

1. I am not rich, so the passage does not apply.
2. I do not covet material things, so the message is irrelevant.
3. I have never behaved like the rich fool.
4. My lifestyle does not reflect a love for the world or desire for "the good life."

Let's address each of these and explore how each represents a fallacy for the majority of us.

The first response requires the right frame of reference. Most of us identify someone richer as our reference point. Irrespective of how wealthy we are, we are never as rich as those wealthier than us. Not surprisingly, we compare ourselves to those who are richer because in a stark one-to-one comparison we convince ourselves we are not wealthy. Employing such comparisons demonstrates the hardness of our hearts and our passion for maintaining our current lifestyle. Our deceit on this initial point represents the first hurdle we must overcome.

The fact is that those in the United States are far richer than most of the world. Much of the world survives on a couple dollars a day income, and the vast majority does not have access to our basic standard of living including indoor plumbing and clean drinking water. They suffer terrible diseases we eradicated long ago in the United States and they have little access to healthcare. Often they live in single room structures of recycled, discarded materials, if they have any place at all.

Moreover, the tremendous global wealth that exists today is unparalleled in human history. We have conveniences that prior generations never imagined (cars, appliances, air conditioning, central heat, mattresses, televisions, cell phones, etc.). The poorest Americans generally have a much higher living standard than many of the wealthy from five hundred, a thousand, or two thousand years ago. Using historical wealth and comparing ourselves to those across the world today represents a more reasonable reference point. In those comparisons almost all of us are wealthy in America; and many of us are obscenely rich.

Second, we often insist we are not covetous, as did the man who asked Jesus to intervene for him regarding an inheritance. Scripture reveals little about him except that he was a part of the crowd and made a single request of Jesus. "Tell my brother to divide the inheritance with me." This man had come to listen to Jesus and he recognized that Jesus spoke with authority, evidenced by his request that Jesus *tell* his brother to share. Evidently, he expected his brother to respect Jesus' perspective due to His wisdom. So he boldly made his request from within the crowd. He had the chance to make one request of Jesus, and what does he seek? He seeks something material. He wants Jesus to intervene in a dispute he has with his brother and decide the issue in his favor.

Notice the man's priority. He focused on the temporal. This man has an opportunity to petition the living God for something and he goes straight for worldly possessions. He pursues that which will benefit him. He makes no spiritual request. He does not ask Jesus to reveal any hidden sin in his life or petition Him for spiritual wisdom or lift up the needs of others. His request does not focus on knowing the Father more closely. Instead he wants to leverage Jesus to acquire more wealth. It is an incredibly selfish demand— "Jesus, tell him to give me what is his." It is not a request as much as a command and it reveals three things about the man: (1) He believes Jesus should fulfill his request; (2) he possesses a selfish heart; (3) and he desires the things of the world.

Too often we come before the Lord in similar fashion. We demand Jesus fulfill our requests. We seek something selfish. We petition for material things of this world.

Lord, tell that company to give me a job.

Lord, tell my boss to give me a raise.

Lord, tell the bank to approve my loan application.

Lord, tell the admission committee to admit me into college.

Lord, tell my debtors to release my debt.

Lord, tell my supervisor to promote me.

Lord, tell my parents to give me a car.

Lord, tell the judge to award me my lawsuit.

Lord, solve this dispute in my favor.

Of course we couch our requests in spiritual terms. We emphasize to God that we will be better Christians if He honors our requests. But in each instance, I imagine Jesus responds to us in a manner similar to the way He did the man in the crowd, "Take heed and beware of covetousness, for one's life does not consist in the abundance of the things he possesses" (Luke 12:15).

At the heart of each of those requests is a form of covetousness. Like the man in the crowd, we focus our requests on ourselves, not on Him or on others. Too often, our petitions reveal:

- We desire to be more like our neighbors rather than more like our Lord.
- We desire to have more of the world rather than more of heaven.
- We desire the temporal, not the eternal.
- We desire the lusts of the flesh, not the fruit of the Spirit.
- We desire God fulfill our will rather than reveal His will.
- We pray through the lens of culture, not through the eyes of Christ.
- We have lifted up self rather than sacrificed self.

Remove the "we" above and replace it with "I" if this improper focus characterizes many of your prayers. It is easy to fall into this temptation and pray according to the flesh, asking the Lord to fulfill our requests as part of His will. I imagine God and His Son weep over the prayer life many of us have. The majority of our prayers focus on self. While we pray some for friends and family, and occasionally pray for the lost, our prayers center on ourselves and our interests too much. This contrasts with the focus God wants for us when we pray.

So return to the question that started this discussion, "Are you covetous?" Your prayer life answers the question. Honestly assess the focus of your prayers. If they emphasize you and worldly things, then they demonstrate a heart of covetousness. If so, humbly ask God's forgiveness and ask Him to rip out the covetous spirit in your heart. Ask Him daily to reveal an area of your life where you continue to covet. He will change your heart over time, and your focus will sharpen in alignment with Him as a result. We will discuss this in more detail in chapter twenty-four.

Third, we convince ourselves we never behave like the rich fool. But we do. Our conduct mirrors his because we share his love for this world. We have filled our homes with so many material things that we now store the excess at a storage facility and pay someone for that privilege. That demonstrates the insatiable appetite we have for material things. We want. We covet. So we purchase and acquire increasing amounts of stuff. Such behavior parallels the conduct of the rich fool. We display with our income the same selfishness he had with his grain. In both instances the focus rests on satisfying self.

But it is not just our use of storage units that display our imitation of the rich fool. We exhibit a mindset of materialism and love for this world in many of our spending decisions:

- We trade in a perfectly good car for a new one.
- We sell a comfortable home and purchase a bigger, nicer one.
- We give perfectly good clothes to charity and then go on a shopping spree.

- We take nice vacations to idyllic locations to relax, because we deserve it.
- We increase our 401(k) contribution to ensure a stable and secure retirement.
- We invest in stocks and money market accounts for use later so we, like the rich fool, can "take our ease; eat, drink, and be merry" (Luke 12:17).

Here is one quick rule of thumb for determining whether you invest in the things of God or simply provide treasure for yourself. As your income has increased over the past five, ten, or twenty-five years, how much has the percentage of your tithe and donations increased? Do not consider the absolute amount since no doubt that increased as your income grew. Instead, determine whether the amount you tithe to church and donate to Christian ministries has increased as a percentage of your income? Has it increased significantly, marginally, remained flat, or declined? Unless it climbed substantively over the years, consider yourself the modern equivalent of the rich fool. You are taking the increase from God and using it to build the modern equivalent of bigger barns. Like the rich fool, you acquire much in this world and achieve considerable success but must confront the same question Jesus posed to His disciples: "For what is a man profited if he gains the whole world and loses his own soul?" (Matthew 16:26)

Fourth, some will say they do not live the lifestyle of the man in this parable. But a careful examination of his comment indicates we may mirror his perspective more closely than we believe. Following his financial success and having invested his windfall for his future, the man reflects on the lifestyle he will now maintain: "I will say to my soul, 'Soul, you have many goods laid up for many years; take your ease; eat, drink, and be merry'" (Luke 12:19).

We learn several characteristics about the man from his comment. First, he focuses on self. He addresses himself in pondering the optimal use of his time in the midst of his financial boon. He adheres to the selfish view that his wealth and goods are *his* alone, for whatever use he deems best. He focuses on *his* future. God is absent from this picture. He fails to recognize God as the provider of his bounty. He neither glorifies God as author of the blessing nor does he offer God thanksgiving for that blessing. Instead, he glorifies and credits himself for his achievements. He revels in his own self-worth, choosing to believe his own hand brought about success. Absent from his consideration are the needs of others. He never considers using God's blessing to help those less fortunate. He expresses no interest in supporting ministries that advance the Great Commission and share the love of Christ with the lost, hurting, and downtrodden.

How often do we adopt this view, believing our hard work, intelligence, and ability produced the success we enjoy at work and in our lives? How easy to forget that God is our provider. We neglect the magnitude of God's role and fail to humbly credit Him for our accomplishments because we have bought into the cultural lie that we earned it. We may talk with others about God's blessing in a generic sense, but too often we neglect to give Him glory for specific achievements, such as when we deliver a great presentation, close a big deal, get promoted, receive a plum new assignment, perform a successful surgery, win a difficult legal case, create a brilliant marketing slogan, receive an 'A' on a difficult exam, obtain employee-of-the-month honors, or receive a favorable annual review.

In these day-to-day wins we tend to credit ourselves and tell others how we achieved our success. In doing so, we demonstrate the attitude and perspective of the rich man in Jesus' parable; we focus our achievements entirely around our own contributions. Paul highlights the error of such thinking. He asks, "Who makes you differ from another? And what do you have that you did not receive? Now if you did indeed receive it, why do you glory as if you had not received it?" (1 Corinthians 4:7). Paul reminds us that every attribute we possess reflects God's design. Every difference in our character, physical attributes, mental acumen, and behavior comes from God Almighty. He created each of us uniquely and equipped us with every characteristic we enjoy.

- God provided your intelligence.
- God bestowed your work ethic.
- God gifted your passion for quality.
- God created your ability to motivate others.
- God blessed your attention to detail.
- God equipped you with a skill for numbers.
- God produced your speed, strength, and agility.
- God fashioned your robust analytic ability.
- God designed your artistic skill.
- God formed your relentless energy to work harder than others.
- God developed your optimistic, engaging personality to network easily.
- God crafted your creativity.

God alone constructed every strength, skill, ability, and attribute you possess. He created you, your personality, and your passions uniquely. He did all this for a specific purpose: for His glory. He desires that we follow His unique plan, honor Him in all we do, recognize His work in us, and testify of Him in all we accomplish. That's right. God has a unique plan for you. Isn't that awesome? What an incredible thought to contemplate—that you are His unique creation and He has a unique plan for your life. That fact reveals an incredible truth: you are special to our Creator.

So what does God think when we take credit for the gifts and abilities He gives us? How does God view our pride when it exalts itself and claims we created our own success? Such arrogance constitutes a rebellion against God because it idolizes self as god. By asserting that we developed our skills and talents, we establish self as our lord. Pride drives that perspective and must be abased, to properly honor the Lord.

Moreover, when we employ these gifts, abilities, and attributes to advance our own agenda and ignore His unique plan for us, we reject His sovereignty. When we use our talents to pursue our goals, we reject His Lordship. Such behavior asserts our plan is better than God's and the destination we identified for our life is superior to His. What an arrogant view. God calls us to use our skills to accomplish the plans He has for us, not to direct them for our own benefit.

We mirror the rich man in Jesus' parable in another way as well, by adopting his perspective in how to live life. On reaching a milestone of success, the rich fool decided it was time to take his "ease; eat, drink, and be merry." Similarly, we achieve some level of success and decide to pursue our own comfort and leisure as well. We begin to pursue more of the good life; relaxing and enjoying the finer things life offers. We pursue whatever brings us happiness and seek out entertainment and pleasure. In such pursuits we parallel our worldly friends and neighbors who have no faith in Christ.

Of course, this perspective demonstrates an inward focus. It evidences our view that the fruit of our success is ours alone, and we can spend as much of it on ourselves as we desire. The rich farmer from the parable held that view—it was his right to seek those things that gave him satisfaction. Since he alone was responsible for his achievements, he alone dictated the use of the benefits they produced. Sadly, we often take the same approach and direct the benefits of our success on lavishing ourselves with the things of this world.

These two perspectives go hand in hand. The one who believes he is largely responsible for his achievements invariably directs the benefits of that success to his own pleasure, comfort, and happiness. In the process, God gets lost. Once we begin down that road, it is very difficult to get off. Why? It is too comfortable, too enjoyable, too alluring.

Sadly, most of us pursue "the good life" and mirror the attitudes of the rich man in Jesus' parable. We believe our success is a product of our efforts and therefore we have the right to spend the fruits of our labor however we please. Too often we spend the majority of those benefits on ourselves and a worldly lifestyle that brings pleasure and happiness. This philosophy is not limited to the wealthy; it impacts Christians across every economic level, "Because from the least of them even to the greatest of them, everyone is given to covetousness" (Jeremiah 6:13). Similarly, most of us have embraced the covetousness, greed, and self-idolatry that mark the "good life."

Living "the good life" has no basis in Scripture. Jesus admonished against it and rhetorically asked, "What is a man profited if he gains the whole world, and loses his own soul?" (Matthew 16:26) The "good life" is a product of our culture. It reflects the American dream and emphasizes our role in our success and teaches that we determine how to enjoy the resulting wealth.

If this lifestyle has no scriptural basis, why do so few sermons explain the danger of living "the good life" and the covetousness it reflects? Why aren't most pastors preaching against the materialism, selfishness, and pride that consume this lifestyle? Why aren't Christian leaders teaching that the good life is an abomination before God? It is because our Christian leaders often have the same sin in their lives. They embrace this perspective and teach that a lifestyle of comfort and pleasure does not conflict with the life of discipleship. Their lifestyles affirm the acceptability of a life emphasizing entertainment, self, and the pursuit of worldly possessions. As a result, American Christianity suffers the same problem Jeremiah observed: "Everyone is given to covetousness, from the prophet even to the priest" (Jeremiah 8:10b). We need to awake to the sin of this lifestyle.

So how should we respond? We must diligently seek God's forgiveness for this perspective. It demonstrates a heart filled with pride and a love of self. In a real sense, our behavior represents idolatry. Ask God to break your heart from such selfishness and remove the pride from your spirit. God desires that such self-consumed conduct no longer have dominion over your life. Identify two actions you can take to begin eliminating covetousness in your life. Ask God for guidance over this decision and the strength to follow through in the days ahead.

1. In what ways does your life mirror the rich fool's? How does God want you to address this?

2. Do you covet? What does your lifestyle suggest? Why is covetousness such a dangerous sin?

3. Do you glorify God with any success He brings you? Do you view the fruits of that success as His or yours? How do your spending habits validate or contradict that response?

Do not love the world or the things in the world. If anyone loves the world, the love of the Father is not in him. For all that is in the world—the lust of the flesh, the lust of the eyes, and the pride of life—is not of the Father but is of the world.

—1 John 2:15-16

CHAPTER 10

Do Not Love the World

A significant inconsistency exists between many of Jesus' teachings and how the American church lives. Our love for the world accounts for much of that contradiction. With all our wealth, unmatched comfort, material possessions, and our lifestyles focused on pleasure and entertainment, we have fallen head over heels in love with this world. Moreover, our culture expects this lifestyle; it bonds us as a nation. Society treats our happiness as a fundamental right. Manufacturers suggest acquiring possessions represents our duty as Americans. Religious leaders explain that our wealth and safety as a nation reflects God's blessing on America. Our entertainment has become an obsession for the media, technology, and athletic industries that collectively reinforce the importance of our leisure. Advertisers convince us to prioritize our comfort and emphasize meeting our desires.

The church, for its part, has acquiesced with this line of thinking. Instead of speaking out against the selfishness, materialism, and idolatry that this worldview promotes, the church has remained silent. The message we hear from most pulpits implies compatibility between the hedonism of the world and following Jesus. Few preachers teach the two are mutually exclusive. Consequently, the church body holds a heretical view that discipleship and worldliness can co-exist. Observing this harmonious partnership between church teaching and worldly priorities leaves society with the impression the two are naturally reconciled.

But Jesus offers a decidedly different view. During His ministry He explained on numerous occasions the danger of adopting the priorities and passions of the world. His parables emphasize the importance of pursuing Him and not the things of this world. But our love for the world blinds us to understanding and accepting Jesus' perspective on these matters. We cannot embrace the truth of God's Word because our arms already embrace the things of the world.

John understood the deadly threat of falling in love with the world. He knew loving the world and all it offers preempts us from loving the Lord and keeping His commands. He warned: "Do not love the world or the things in the world. If anyone loves the world, the love of the Father is not in him. For all that is in the world—the lust of the flesh, the lust of the eyes, and the pride of life—is not of the Father but is of the world" (1 John 2:15-16).

John asserts an important fact: anyone who loves the world does not possess genuine faith. Authentic faith yields the presence of the Holy Spirit, who produces the love of the Father. Yet John states God's love does not exist in anyone who loves this world or the things in it. The two are irreconcilable. We may want to believe otherwise, but Scripture does not equivocate on the issue. So we have a choice: love the Lord or love the world. Love the difficult life as a disciple of Jesus or love the pleasure, possessions, and comfort of this world.

Conceptually, the decision poses no difficulty. All who profess faith in Christ will claim they love Jesus. Applying that truth substantively in our lives presents a more difficult proposition, especially when it requires rejecting the lures of this world. We must understand the critical distinction between not loving the world and claiming not to love it. John admonishes us to avoid loving the world and the things in it, not simply disclaiming a love for this world. Our affirmation must translate into action.

A love for this world destroys the faith of individual believers and diminishes the power and effectiveness of the local church.

Let me provide an example. A pastor from Eastern Europe shared how the size of his congregation declined dramatically over the two decades following the end of the Cold War. The decline contrasted remarkably with the growth and vibrancy his church experienced under communist rule when the church had to meet in secret to avoid arrest and torture. In describing why the church had thrived under the iron fist of Communism, while weakening under a free and democratic society experiencing tremendous economic growth, the pastor said, "We survived persecution, but we could not survive prosperity."

How profound. Let's reflect on that insight for a minute. How could the church thrive in an environment so hostile to faith and which put believers at risk of jail or violence and then, in contrast, decline severely once freedom arrived and believers could worship openly? I imagine the church thrived under communism for several reasons. First, faith provided hope to a people with little hope in this world. So they placed their hope in the eternal. Sure, this life was horrible, but they looked forward to eternity with Jesus, when all their tears and pain would disappear and they could rest in the presence of God. More importantly though, I think the church thrived because faith cost something in that environment. Like those in Jesus' parables, Christians under communism had to count the cost before committing to Christ. And they did. When they learned of the mercy of God through Jesus, they willingly gave up everything. Sure, it might result in jail or a beating, but salvation from the living God and a relationship with Jesus was worth any price. While faith cost something, it offered everything in return.

In addition, life under communism presented little material distraction. Believers under communism did not love the world or the things of the world because they had so little and what they did own was unimpressive. Without distractions from the world's treasures, believers could spend more time growing in faith, in prayer, learning God's word, and fellowshipping with one another because those activities brought them joy and peace. As they spent more time drawing close to God their faith matured. Their maturity developed in them boldness and steadfastness to withstand the threats and persecution from the government. That resilience, in turn, drew more people to the church, who wanted desperately the purpose and strength they saw in those believers.

Something similar exists in many developing countries today where wealth rarely exists. Christianity enjoys its most explosive growth today in places where little temporal or material distraction exists. In fact, Christianity thrives where the cost to practice faith is high.

In contrast, American believers often seek momentary gratification by pursuing the thrills of this world, in concert with our unbelieving peers. But our worldly pursuits impose a tremendous cost on our faith and on the local church. Our frenetic quest for the good life and acquisition of the world's treasures invariably leads to love. We won't admit it. But it does. Passion for the things of the world always leads to love. It represents an equation as factual as 2+2=4. You cannot spend significant time pursuing and enjoying the things of this world without falling in love. No amount of protest changes that fact. Our love for the world, then, precludes a love for the Father. John provides no exception nor offers a middle-ground for compromise. Listen to him again: "If anyone loves the world, the love of the Father is not in him" (1 John 2:15).

John's declaration should lead each of us to examine his heart, carefully considering whether a love for the world exists. Each of us ought to ask God to reveal the true state of his heart. Unfortunately, many of us will dismiss the possibility that we love the world, affirming that we only love the Lord. However, such a cavalier disavowal reveals the heart's hardness and demonstrates how resistant it is to the truth.

Similarly, the Eastern European church declined after its nation began thriving economically. Believers fell in love with the world and no longer loved the Father. They decided to quit wasting time pretending to be something they weren't: the Lord's.

Recall Jesus' words in His sermon on the mount: "No one can serve two masters; for either he will hate the one and love the other, or else he will be loyal to the one and despise the other. You cannot serve God and mammon [money, power]" (Matthew 6:24). Jesus states a fact we would do well to meditate on as a church. It is not a remote chance. It is not a possibility. It is not even highly likely. It is an indisputable fact. No one can love both God and the world. No one can love the fruit of the Spirit and the riches of the world. They are mutually exclusive. You can love one, or be loyal to the other, but never both.

James echoes this truth, asking, "Do you not know that friendship with the world is enmity with God? Whoever therefore wants to be a friend of the world makes himself an enemy of God" (James 4:4). We can friend God or we can friend the world, but you cannot friend both. The flesh resists this truth. It fights back when learning what God's Word says about the world—that you cannot love it as a disciple of Christ. In response your flesh tells you things like the following:

- I do not love the world.
- I do not love the things of the world.
- I only love God.
- I put God first.
- He is first in how I allocate time.
- He is first in how I spend money.
- I may dabble in the things of the world, but I certainly do not love it.

You rationalize your lifestyle and choices:

- Yes, I possess lots of worldly stuff.
- Yes, I spend most of my free time pursuing leisure, pleasure, and entertainment.
- Yes, I spend more time shopping than studying God's word.
- Yes, I spend more time watching television than in prayer to God.
- Sure, I love going online, playing games, and updating my social-media pages.

- Sure, I rarely spend time with the needy and hurting in our communities.
- Sure, my priorities reflect a love for the world, not God.
- Sure, my time demonstrates a love for the world, not God.
- Okay, I spend money disproportionately for my comfort than advancing God's kingdom.
- Sure, my life mirrors my non-Christian neighbors more than Jesus'.
- Nevertheless, I do *not* love the world or the things in it.

We tell ourselves that nonsense and convince ourselves that despite all evidence to the contrary, we have no love for this world. Perhaps you are telling yourself that right now. Your flesh wants you to believe that lie. It will seek to convince you that you love God and not the world. Why? Because once you realize you love the world, you will take immediate and substantive steps to change your heart. You will seek God's forgiveness and ask Him to begin removing your love for this world.

If our relationship with Jesus was as close as we claim, we would easily identify the disparity between what we claim to love and the reality. That disconnect between truth—evidenced by our behavior, decisions, and lifestyle—and what we profess to believe does a serious disservice to the name of Jesus. Worse, that inconsistency signals to the culture that covetousness, materialism, selfishness, and worldliness are acceptable behaviors. It suggests that such conduct does not constitute sin. From observing our lifestyles, society learns that temporal things matter most, which validates their own priorities with the world. Our lifestyles obfuscate the culture's understanding of its need for the Savior. It may even conceal our own need for the Savior.

You may struggle with these truths; they are indeed difficult to accept. They are even more difficult to apply. I encourage you to seek God's wisdom as you discuss the questions with others who earnestly desire to follow the Lord. Hold each other accountable on the changes you commit to make in your life and encourage each other in your efforts.

1. Why does John tell us not to love the world?

2. Jesus says we cannot love both God and the world. Why is it impossible to love both?

3. In what areas of your life do you demonstrate a love for the world? What action(s) do you commit to taking to begin eliminating your love for the world?

Present your bodies a living sacrifice, holy, acceptable to God, which is your reasonable service. And do not be conformed to this world, but be transformed by the renewing of your mind, that you may prove what is that good and acceptable and perfect will of God.

—Romans 12:1-2

CHAPTER 11

Do Not Conform to the World

This world constantly attempts to persuade the believer to become friends and enjoy the pleasures and possessions it offers. It does not require we renounce our faith as part of the agreement. Society merely requires recalibrating our faith to align with its standards. To achieve harmony with the culture, we need only live a faith the world finds palatable. Of course, any such concession invariably dilutes the faith of the believer. Such compromise yields ineffective and unfocused Christians at best and carnal, faux Christians at worst. Either result pleases the world, though it prefers the latter scenario. Remember that Satan is the god of this age and God has given him dominion over Earth until the Lord returns. He is the one wanting us to compromise our faith.

Until Christ returns, Satan remains on the hunt. He seeks to destroy the people of God and prevent others from developing a personal relationship with Jesus. One of his most effective tools appeals to our lust for this world, enticing believers into compromise. Through media, television programs, entertainers, friends, opinion influencers, and thought leaders, the world incessantly challenges us to bargain with our faith. Society casts doubt on the standards of God and ridicules the teachings of Jesus. It marginalizes those who follow Christ as a disciple and holds with contempt any who pursue holiness and obedience to

God. It preaches a message of tolerance for all manner of sin but derides as outdated anything from God.

But God rejects such nonsense. He advises that we not conform to the world. We must resist the temptation to submit to the world's standards. Paul encourages believers to "present your bodies a living sacrifice, holy, acceptable to God, which is your reasonable service. And do not be conformed to this world, but be transformed by the renewing of your mind, that you may prove what is that good and acceptable and perfect will of God" (Romans 12:1-2).

As disciples of Jesus, Paul tells us to offer our bodies to the Lord as a sacrifice. In response to His physical sacrifice for us that led to His death, we present ourselves to Him as a living sacrifice, holy consecrated for His work. Such sacrifice changes how we live. We cannot continue to chase the lifestyle we had before committing our lives to Him. Instead our thoughts, speech, and conduct begin to mirror those of the Lord. Our thoughts become more pure. Our speech loses its vulgarity and we avoid gossip. Our behavior becomes godlier as we avoid licentious acts.

Our transformation comes from the Holy Spirit and springs from our desire to please God because of His favor and the salvation He provides. Paul says that our transformation does not represent a Herculean task that only the pious pursue. Rather, it is the reasonable response of every believer. Every person who experiences God's mercy should dedicate his life for God's glory. He gave His life for our eternal salvation; giving our life for His glory is our reasonable response.

That transformation precludes conforming to the world. When the world requests compromise, we must resist. Conforming to its standards and adopting its priorities runs counter to the will of God. Instead, our transformation to God's ways allows us to demonstrate a more compelling witness to the world. Our lives point to the Father and the will He has established for this world. As a consequence, God uses us to transform the lives of those around us.

Peter articulates this connection between godly conduct and serving as God's witness to our community of friends and family. "Beloved, I beg you as sojourners and pilgrims, abstain from fleshly lusts which war against the soul, having your conduct honorable among the Gentiles, that when they speak against you as evildoers, they may, by your good works which they observe, glorify God in the day of visitation" (1 Peter 2:11-12). Echoing Paul's challenge to avoid ungodly lusts and conduct, Peter encourages us to live in a manner that brings God glory even in the midst of idle chatter and contempt from society.

Peter builds on the transformation theme later in the epistle, adding an emphasis of urgency to the task. He informs us that the world will think you odd and foolish in choosing God's transformation rather than conforming to the world. "Therefore, since Christ suffered for us in the flesh, arm yourselves also with the same mind, for he who has suffered in the flesh has ceased from sin, that he no longer should live the rest of his time in the flesh for the lusts of men, but for the will of God. For we have spent enough of our past lifetime in doing the will of the Gentiles—when we walked in licentiousness, lusts, drunkenness, revelries, drinking parties, and abominable idolatries. In regard to these, they think it strange that you do not run with them in the same flood of dissipation, speaking evil of you. They will give an account to Him who is ready to judge the living and the dead" (1 Peter 4:1-5).

Peter correctly points out that in coming to Christ we ought to adopt His perspective. Our lives should not reflect a lifestyle of sin that mirrors the unbeliever. Instead, we should pursue the will of God. A dramatic difference should contrast our former life with our current life. Peter then reminds us that we have wasted too much of our lives pursuing this world. We have invested too much time living in sin and doing the will of our friends, neighbors, colleagues, and family. Peer pressure and compromise led us to choices that the world approved but which disobeyed God. We allowed our desire for popularity to cloud our judgment, leading to all kinds of shameful conduct: wild parties, drunk-fests, sexual perversions, materialism, and other hedonistic behavior.

Irrespective of when you became a believer, you spent too much time living the way of the world and pursuing sin prior to your conversion. Even those who come to the Lord at a young age share the same spirit of rebellion and compromise that leads to the aforementioned behavior. Consequently, our thoughts, conduct, activities, and relationships were all directed toward what was best for us. In each area, we made decisions that advanced our agenda but ignored God. Nothing we did or thought had eternal value; it focused entirely on the temporal. So Peter tells us to transform ourselves to the mind of Christ and cease the old lifestyle that appealed to the world. He discourages us from wasting any more time on sinful behavior.

Keep in mind, though, that the world will ridicule you for your changed behavior. When you refuse to participate in the sins you formerly committed, they will direct epitaphs and abuse at you. They will mock your faith, find your new lifestyle boring, and be judgmental. But Peter encourages us to remain steadfast in our new faith and maintain the life of godliness that God has called us to live, even at the expense of our friends and colleagues. They will have to give an account, he tells us, of their behavior and will suffer eternally for their abuse. In view of that, do not allow their verbal assaults to discourage you or cause you to compromise.

Having wasted our pre-conversion lives, we must redeem the time now. Paul says, "See then that you walk circumspectly, not as fools but as wise, redeeming the time because the days are evil" (Ephesians 5:15-16). We must spend what remains of our life on Earth pursuing those activities and attributes that bring God glory. Yes, they will think you odd and call you names, but you must mirror Christ and not the world.

So, how do we avoid the temptations of this world? How do we resist the lure of our prior lifestyle when friends call and peers pressure us? How do we maintain the mind of Christ and not slip back into our previous sinful behavior? Paul provides sound counsel on this issue. He encouraged Timothy: "Flee also youthful lusts; but pursue righteousness, faith, love, peace with those who call on the Lord out of a pure heart" (2 Timothy 2:22). An ideal way to avoid temptation is to avoid those situations that tempt. If you are tempted to get overly physical with your significant other, quit starting the physical behavior at any level.

If you are tempted to view pornography, have someone install filtering software and not give you the access code. If drunkenness haunts you, quit going out with your drinking buddies. Flee the sinful behavior but also flee those environments that tempt us to sin.

However, fleeing sin is insufficient. Paul challenged Timothy to also pursue those attributes that God calls us to possess, including righteousness. He made a similar comment in his first epistle to Timothy, telling him: "Flee these things and pursue righteousness, godliness, faith, love, patience, gentleness" (1 Timothy 6:11). Daily pursuing the attributes of Jesus will make it difficult for sin to gain a foothold in your life. Moreover, seek these qualities with other believers who share your love for the Lord and desire to obey Him. Genuine fellowship sharpens the faith of each participating disciple of Christ. Having brothers and sisters in the Lord who will challenge and encourage you in your faith journey is a tremendous blessing; make sure you seek such fellowship.

Paul provides another path for avoiding temptation. "[T]hat the righteous requirement of the law might be fulfilled in us who do not walk according to the flesh but according to the Spirit. For those who live according to the flesh set their minds on the things of the flesh, but those who live according to the Spirit, the things of the Spirit. For to be carnally minded is death, but to be spiritually minded is life and peace. Because the carnal mind is enmity against God; for it is not subject to the law of God, nor indeed can be. So then, those who are in the flesh cannot please God. But you are not in the flesh but in the Spirit, if indeed the Spirit of God dwells in you. Now if anyone does not have the Spirit of Christ, he is not His" (Romans 8:4-9).

Set your mind on the Spirit. Those who do will walk according to the Spirit, which means they will live in accordance with the principles of God. Avoiding wickedness requires more than our passive avoidance of sin, we must actively pursue the Spirit. As our minds focus on Him we lose our desire to pursue dishonorable behavior. God replaces our tendency towards sin with a yearning for Him, as we meditate on His Spirit. Paul reminds us that the Spirit of God dwells in us, if indeed we are His. We demonstrate His presence as we seek those things above which represent the character of God, and put on His attributes that we learn about as we study His Word.

God calls us to a transformed life. The life of every believer should contrast significantly with the world. We must encourage each other to remain steadfast in pursuing conduct that mirrors Jesus rather than aligns with the world's standards. Avoid those situations that provide the strongest temptation, and instead pursue fellowship with other believers. As you do, you will become a living sacrifice for God.

1. Are there areas in your life that conform to the world? If so, what will you do to allow God to transform that area so it aligns with His will?

2. Why do people find it so easy to conform to the world, its standards, expectations, and lusts?

3. Can you think of why the world responds with such vitriol, ridicule, and contempt for believers when we seek to follow God's way instead of society's?

He also said to His disciples: "There was a certain rich man who had a steward, and an accusation was brought to him that this man was wasting his goods. So he called him and said to him, 'What is this I hear about you? Give an account of your stewardship, for you can no longer be steward.' Then the steward said within himself, 'What shall I do? For my master is taking the stewardship away from me. I cannot dig; I am ashamed to beg. I have resolved what to do, that when I am put out of the stewardship, they may receive me into their houses.' So he called every one of his master's debtors to him, and said to the first, 'How much do you owe my master?' And he said, 'A hundred measures of oil.' So he said to him, 'Take your bill, and sit down quickly and write fifty.' Then he said to another, 'And how much do you owe?' So he said, 'A hundred measures of wheat.' And he said to him, 'Take your bill, and write eighty.' So the master commended the unjust steward because he had dealt shrewdly. For the sons of this world are more shrewd in their generation than the sons of light. And I say to you, make friends for yourselves by unrighteous mammon, that when you fail, they may receive you into an everlasting home. He who is faithful in what is least is faithful also in much; and he who is unjust in what is least is unjust also in much. Therefore if you have not been faithful in the unrighteous mammon, who will commit to your trust the true riches? And if you have not been faithful in what is another man's, who will give you what is your own? "No servant can serve two masters; for either he will hate the one and love the other, or else he will be loyal to the one and despise the other. You cannot serve God and mammon." Now the Pharisees, who were lovers of money, also heard all these things, and they derided Him. And He said to them, "You are those who justify yourselves before men, but God knows your hearts. For what is highly esteemed among men is an abomination in the sight of God.

—Luke 16:1-15

CHAPTER 12

Dangers of Wealth

Another way we avoid the difficult path involves our pursuit of wealth. Wealth provides a level of comfort we cherish and minimizes the hardship we experience in this world. However, it also prevents us from fully trusting the Lord, teaching us to put our faith in money, not God.

Scripture addresses wealth on many occasions and a warning of some sort almost always accompanies the message. In one instance, Jesus observed, "How hard it is for those who have riches to enter the kingdom of God! For it is easier for a camel to go through a needle's eye than for a rich man to enter the kingdom of God" (Luke 18:24-25). How often do we hear our pastors preach on these verses and warn us of the dangers of pursuing wealth? Not often enough, and when they are addressed too often the pastor explains away the scriptural truth. When teaching about wealth, too many pastors explain why applicable Scripture does not mean what it appears to mean. For example, with respect to the above verses we often hear that Jesus is not teaching us that the wealthy have difficulty entering heaven. Yet that is exactly what He tells us; His words leave no room for misinterpretation.

So why do pastors avoid addressing biblical truth regarding wealth and the pursuit of riches? There are several reasons. First, most of us have little interest in hearing the message. We want to enjoy the riches of this world while simultaneously professing faith in Christ. Biblical warnings against accumulating wealth cramp our lifestyles and contradict our narrative that God wants to bless us with material possessions.

Second, pastors who preach the truth on wealth and materialism likely will confront a dwindling congregation. Some members and regular attendees will leave for a church that does not challenge them on the issue. Rather than risk that outcome many pastors avoid the subject altogether, or choose to explain relevant passages in a way that reinforces our desire to embrace both the comforts of wealth and the call of Christ. Consequently, most churches present an unbiblical position on matters of prosperity. In fact, the prevailing view of the church regarding riches and faith generally falls into one or both of the following positions:

1. The Lord materially blesses those who love Him and keep His commands, and therefore wealth reflects God's favor for living a Christian life.
2. Verses addressing the danger of wealth and materialism require our intellectual agreement but do not require substantive, sacrificial application in our lives.

Rather than blindly follow the predominant teaching on this subject, we need to investigate what Scripture says and understand how it contrasts with the beliefs and practices of the American church. Consider the parable of the unjust steward at the beginning of the chapter. Jesus concludes the parable by remarking that we cannot serve God and the world. Either we faithfully distribute the riches He gives us according to His priorities, or we lavish them on ourselves. If we claim to serve God but then direct His bounty in support of our lifestyles we deceive ourselves. Spending wealth on our own desires demonstrates poor stewardship and reveals our belief that we own our assets rather than having a stewardship relationship with the true owner, God. It is His money and He asks us to distribute it as good stewards. How do we faithfully administer that stewardship, spending His wealth on ourselves or on kingdom purposes?

Jesus warns, "Therefore, if you have not been faithful in the unrighteous mammon (worldly wealth), who will commit to your trust the true riches?" (Luke 16:11). Failing to faithfully invest His gifts reveals our love for the world. As a result, we have no role in administering the true riches of heaven because we inappropriately distributed the wealth He provided in this world. God tests in this world our obedience to His commands on stewardship before He entrusts us with genuine valuables in heaven. Curiously, many of us disobey His principles, choosing to enjoy His wealth in this world and forfeit our entitlement to future riches in heaven. It is a trade-off that makes no sense unless you do not believe Jesus' promise of the treasures to come, which He described as the true riches. While He never explains in detail what those true riches are, they will certainly surpass in magnificence anything we have on Earth. So why do most of us settle for scraps in the here and now?

In response to Jesus' parable and warning, Luke tells us, "Now the Pharisees, who were lovers of money, also heard all these things, and they derided Him" (Luke 16:14). The Pharisees had no interest in Jesus' teaching on stewardship. They enjoyed all the benefits their wealth provided and had no intention to change, because they loved money. Upon hearing Jesus' instruction on generosity and sacrificial giving, they ridiculed and mocked Him. What ridiculous principles, they thought. We tithe according to what the Torah requires, why would we give more than that? They adhered to the minimum requirement of the law in outward obedience to God, but retained a spirit of selfishness.

Too often we echo the Pharisees response. We are lovers of money (no matter how much we protest) and likely scoff at the message Jesus stresses. Our love is evidenced by our contentment in purchasing possessions we desire, while tremendous financial needs exist for advancing the gospel across the world. Instead of giving more toward God's work, we prefer spending more on another of our lusts. Our spending behavior illustrates our disinterest in fulfilling the Great Commission and a heart that parallels the Pharisees in retaining a spirit of selfishness.

Most of us actually believe that investing in ourselves represents good stewardship of God's money. We disdain those who suggest we spend more income on kingdom purposes and less on self. We bristle at the suggestion and respond that we already give generously, even though we could give so much more. Too many of us simply give our financial leftovers after funding our consumerist lifestyles. Our giving rarely hurts because we have convinced ourselves that our income belongs to us. But Jesus never tells us to carve out a small portion of our income for Him and then lavish ourselves with the rest. He requires sacrificial giving from us.

In response to the Pharisees derision, Jesus said to them, "You are those who justify yourselves before men, but God knows your hearts. For what is highly esteemed among men is an abomination in the sight of God" (Luke 16:15). We should take heed of that warning. Like the Pharisees, we often attempt to *justify ourselves* before men, including our:

- Lifestyles.
- Materialism.
- Spending habits.
- Pursuit of comfort.
- Absence of sacrificial giving.
- Covetousness.
- Love for the things of this world.

Perhaps you are justifying yourself in some of these areas as you read through this book. As the truth of Scripture burdens your heart, you begin to explain why you already obey God on these topics. If studying in a group, you might agree with each other that your lifestyles align to the Lord's commands. For too long, though, believers have justified themselves on matters of stewardship, wealth, and sacrifice, and fallen further from Christ in the process. But God knows your heart and is not persuaded by your arguments justifying how you administer the income He provides. The second half of that verse identifies a primary reason for our failure to faithfully follow God's commands on these subjects. Pursuing wealth, accumulating possessions, and lifestyles of comfort represent the pinnacles of success we highly esteem. But they are abominations before God. He hates these things because they breed selfishness and distract people from their relationship with Him.

In our pursuit of these things we reveal a covetous nature. We desire the things of the world and direct out efforts to securing them. In chasing those things with such zeal we do more than serve as poor stewards of the resources God provides. We demonstrate a love that approaches worship. Our passion for the things of this world leads to a devotion and reverence we should reserve only for God. Paul informs us what this behavior represents: "Therefore, put to death . . . covetousness, which is idolatry" (Colossians 3:5). He equates our coveting the things of this world with idolatry.

Take a minute and digest this critical truth. As we desire the things of this world, we establish them as our God. By persistently pursuing possessions, our hearts become consumed with them. We prioritize them in our life. This conduct represents covetousness. Our coveting reflects idolatry, which is worshipping a false god. None of us want to admit or even consider that our materialist and consumerist behavior reveals idolatry. We associate that with heathens in faraway countries who worship gods of stone and wood. But we are doing the same, except our gods are made of linen, cotton, metal, and plastic. Our focus and spending demonstrate our true love, and it is not the Lord but "stuff." We love and worship possessions.

So how should we invest the income and wealth God provides us? We need to direct it on His will, fulfilling the Great Commission, and meeting the needs of the least of these (See Matthew 25:31-40). The first-century church provides an excellent example of this. "And they continued steadfastly in the apostles' doctrine and fellowship, in the breaking of bread, and in prayers. Then fear came upon every soul, and many wonders and signs were done through the apostles. Now all who believed were together, and had all things in common, and sold their possessions and goods, and divided them among all, as anyone had need. So continuing daily with one accord in the temple, and breaking bread from house to house, they ate their food with gladness and simplicity of heart, praising God and having favor with all the people. And the Lord added to the church daily those who were being saved" (Acts 2:42-47).

The wealthy shared with the less fortunate brethren so all goods were common for all. This behavior glorified God and attracted others to faith since it showed a selfless love. They held that view because they were growing in the faith by continuing in doctrine, fellowship, and prayer. Mature Christians do this. God honors such generosity by allowing churches to flourish when they adopt it.

Here is another example of the early church sacrificing for the needs of the brethren. "And in these days prophets came from Jerusalem to Antioch. Then one of them, named Agabus, stood up and showed by the Spirit that there was going to be a great famine throughout all the world, which also happened in the days of Claudius Caesar. Then the disciples, each according to his ability, determined to send relief to the brethren dwelling in Judea. This they also did, and sent it to the elders by the hands of Barnabas and Saul" (Acts 11:27-30). Similar needs exist today for brethren across the globe, often of an even larger magnitude. Why do so many of us ignore these needs?

John answers that question in the form of a stern warning for any believer who responds with indifference to the needs of his brethren. "Whoever has this world's goods and sees his brother in need and shuts up his heart from him, how does the love of God abide in him?" (1 John 3:17). John conveys three important truths.

1. Seeing our brethren in need should move us to respond with compassion. More than just offering encouragement, we need to address the need with the resources God has provided.
2. Our response demonstrates the condition of our heart. John identifies those who shut their hearts to the needy as having an absence of love. He does not refer to such individuals as those who shut their wallets. The unwillingness to open your wallet or give other relevant resources is the symptom. The problem, though, lies

in an unwillingness to open your heart. Generosity flows from the heart, as does greed and selfishness.

3. Those who shut their hearts to the needs of the brethren do not possess the love of God. God's love resides in the heart of each believer. God requires we meet the needs of others with the resources He gives us. When we refuse, we reveal His absence from our heart.

As we conclude this chapter, consider the counsel Paul gives Timothy on how the wealthy ought to behave. "Command those who are rich in this present age not to be haughty, nor to trust in uncertain riches but in the living God, who gives us richly all things to enjoy. Let them do good, that they be rich in good works, ready to give, willing to share, storing up for themselves a good foundation for the time to come, that they may lay hold on eternal life" (1 Timothy 6:17-19). Paul's guidance communicates several important points we need to absorb into our lifestyle and faith.

First, those with resources should not adopt an attitude of arrogance. Do not presume you are better than the less fortunate, or that your hands created your wealth. God created us all equal, and your economic status comes from Him, not your hard work.

Second, do not trust your riches to meet your needs. God meets all our needs, and we need to trust in Him alone. Paul reminds us that the riches of this world are uncertain and can disappear overnight (just ask any investor after the housing market collapsed).

Third, use your resources to commit good works that meet the needs of others. Have a willing heart to share with the needy, and do so with a spirit of kindness.

Fourth, store up treasure in heaven which lasts for eternity. Meeting the needs of others, displaying sacrificial generosity, and completing good works all have their reward in heaven.

R. Roderick Cyr

QUESTIONS:

1. Why does God commit true riches only to those who were faithful stewards on Earth?

2. In what areas has God vested you stewardship of His resources? Are you faithfully administering those resources? What action will you take today to become a better steward?

3. Paul equates covetousness with idolatry. Do you agree? Do you display a covetous heart? What specific steps will you implement to eliminate covetousness from your life?

Now as He was going out on the road, one came running, knelt before Him, and asked Him, "Good Teacher, what shall I do that I may inherit eternal life?" So Jesus said to him, "Why do you call Me good? No one is good but One, that is, God. You know the commandments: 'Do not commit adultery,' 'Do not murder,' 'Do not steal,' 'Do not bear false witness,' 'Do not defraud,' 'Honor your father and your mother.'" And he answered and said to Him, "Teacher, all these things I have kept from my youth." Then Jesus, looking at him, loved him, and said to him, "One thing you lack: Go your way, sell whatever you have and give to the poor, and you will have treasure in heaven; and come, take up the cross, and follow Me." But he was sad at this word, and went away grieved, for he had great possessions.

—Mark 10:17-22

CHAPTER 13

Rich Young Ruler

Many of us are familiar with the story of the rich young ruler. He had achieved success by just about any measure used by the world. He had power, influence, and considerable wealth. And he had achieved it at a young age. However, having it all in this life did not satisfy him; he wanted it all in the next life also. He sought to live in the lap of luxury here and now and then transition into eternity and enjoy all the blessings of God there as well. So when he heard Jesus was in town, he made his way to Him to inquire about what it would take to inherit eternal life (Mark 10:17).

Although Scripture does not confirm, I suspect the young ruler did not anticipate learning anything new from Jesus' response. I doubt he expected Jesus to require any change in his life. He probably believed he could encounter the Son of God face to face and walk away unchanged; that he could experience God's presence and not undergo a transformation. He likely assumed he already had a right relationship with God. After all, he had evidence of God's blessing: the wealth, the power, and the prestige. In all likelihood he simply wanted Jesus to confirm what he already knew, that he was a righteous young man well on his way to heaven. And he wanted this affirmation in front of the masses, so he could impress everyone with his faith. Those were likely his expectations.

As Jesus started to respond, he probably thought his plan was playing out as desired; his friends would see he was a man of God. "You know the commandments: 'Do not commit adultery,' 'Do not murder,' 'Do not steal,' 'Do not bear false witness,' 'Do not defraud,' 'Honor your father and your mother'" (Mark 10:19). The young man was ecstatic. He had hoped Jesus would say something along those lines. And so he responds to Jesus, confident that his fulfillment of those requirements would seal his eternal destination in heaven, "Teacher, all these I have observed from my youth" (Mark 10:20).

In many ways we are a lot like this young ruler. We believe we are much holier than we actually are and that we follow God's Word much more closely than we actually do. He believed he was doing God's will in his life and that he really had a love for God. But Jesus knew the condition of his heart, the young ruler's love for God paled in comparison to his love for the world. Jesus observed the inconsistency between what the young man professed with his mouth and what he really believed with his heart.

And so Jesus tells the young man he only lacks one thing to get into heaven: "Go your way, sell whatever you have, and give to the poor, and you will have treasure in heaven; and come, take up the cross and follow Me" (Mark 10:21). The young man, we are told, "went away grieved" (Mark 10:22). Why was the young ruler grieved? Scripture tells us it was because "he had great possessions."

He loved his possessions and the temporal toys of this world more than he loved God and the eternal blessings of the next. Jesus knew the priorities of his heart and the contradiction between what he claimed and reality. The young ruler professed to love God but in actuality loved this world. The blessings he thought were from God and reflected his righteousness were in reality a stumbling block that kept him from following God at all; they blocked his path to salvation. The message from Jesus is clear: do not love this world nor pursue the things of this world, for they preclude a robust, authentic relationship with the Lord.

Surprisingly, many pastors and laymen hold a much different perspective on what Jesus teaches in this passage. The most common view asserts that God is not telling us we need to sell everything; we simply need to have a willingness to sell everything. The wisdom Jesus hopes to convey, according to this view, is that believers *be willing* to sacrifice the material to follow Him. We believe this lie because it reinforces the validity of our lifestyle. Far too many of us have fallen in love with the world and its possessions, and we want to maintain our stuff. We refuse to consider the possibility that God calls us to the same action he called the rich ruler, despite the fact that our lives mirror his in terms of how we handle wealth. In essence, we are the rich young ruler. Each of us.

I am the rich young ruler.

You are the rich young ruler.

God almost certainly is calling each of us to give away many, or most, or maybe all of our possessions and come follow Him. He wants us to direct much more of our resources to spreading the good news of Jesus across the globe and rid ourselves from the covetousness that has kept us from Him. Our resistance and refusal reveals a heart of greed and selfishness, just as it did in the rich ruler. God wants to liberate us from the shackles of the world's goods, which keep us from experiencing a life of joy and satisfaction in fully following Him.

But we reject His truth. We decline to wrestle with the challenge Jesus gave the rich ruler or make any effort to understand what application it might have in our lives. We refuse to consider the possibility that the command Jesus gave the rich ruler is the same command He gives us because it would severely impact our lives, and we would prefer not to deal with such a disruptive event.

Most of us share the condition of the young ruler's heart regarding wealth and possessions. We share his confidence of a healthy relationship with God and a consistent obedience to His Word. Like him, it never occurs to us that our heart is far removed from God. But the ruler's confidence misled him into overstating his commitment to God and obedience to His commands. Recall his response to Jesus' initial advice: "*All* these [commands] I have observed from my youth." He actually believed he had kept all God's commands throughout his life. The arrogance of his claim reflected his true spiritual condition. He pride deceived him so fully that his actual relationship with God was almost non-existent—the opposite of what he believed.

Sadly, that represents the spiritual condition many of us possess in America. Deceived, we believe we have a robust relationship with the Lord and obey His commands. But we evidence the true condition of our relationship in our unwillingness to consider any Scripture that makes our lives more difficult. We want no part of that truth. We want a close relationship with God, but on our terms, not His. So we explain away Jesus' challenge to the young ruler; the insight, we claim, involves our "willingness" to sacrifice and not in actually sacrificing. Jesus simply wants an intellectual affirmation that we will obey and follow Him if He ever demands it, which of course He never does.

But is that what Jesus told the rich young ruler, "be *willing* to go and sell all you have and be *willing* to give to the poor"? If He had made that pronouncement to the ruler, do you know how the young man would have responded? He would have said the same thing we tell ourselves when we read the passage with that interpretation. "I am willing, Lord." The young man would have had no hesitation with being "willing" to sell his property and possessions. He was more than willing. Well, not quite. His problem was with the *actual* selling of his goods and foregoing his wealth as Jesus commanded. Similarly, we are "willing" to obey God in sacrificing everything that interferes in our relationship with Him; we just never actually sacrifice everything. Unless verbal affirmation translates into substantive action, any commitment to God is merely lip service.

In many ways, the story of the rich, young ruler should resonate with most of us. We possess comparable hearts with respect to what we own. Like him, we love wealth and the comfort it provides. We want to love God as well, but we do not want to choose between the two. We prefer a faith that allows us to love both. We want to follow Jesus within reasonable parameters, and we believe it unreasonable to deny ourselves the riches, comfort, and pleasures of this world. But Jesus does not call halfhearted disciples. He will not share with this world the loyalties and love of His followers. He wants complete loyalty and requires undivided love. If you listen, you can hear Him calling out: "Go and sell your possessions, take up your cross and come follow Me."

1. What is your response to the parable of the rich young ruler?

2. How could the rich young ruler believe he had such a healthy relationship with God and yet fail to obey Jesus' command to sell what he owned?

3. Why does God call us to rid ourselves of the wealth and comfort that distract us from Him?

Now he who received seed among the thorns is he who hears the word, and the cares of this world and the deceitfulness of riches choke the word, and he becomes unfruitful.

—Matthew 13:22

CHAPTER 14

Beware the Cares of this World

In this verse from the parable of the sower, Jesus explains why some believers fail to bear fruit. He identifies the "cares of this world" as an obstacle in contributing to the kingdom of God. On initially hearing His Word we receive it with gladness and want to apply it in our lives. But later, we stagnate and cease to grow in our faith. Our spiritual growth stalls because we buy into the deceit of riches and the cares of this world. They corrode our relationship with God and choke His Word, so it no longer has its perfect work in our lives. We must realize that chasing the cares of this world always leads to weakened faith. How do "the cares of this world" make us unfruitful for God?

- They distract us from Jesus.
- They shape our priorities.
- They command our time.
- They dictate our focus.
- They influence our decisions.
- They cloud our judgment.
- They diminish our passion for the Lord.
- They drive our agenda.

As a result, the "cares of the world" impact our lives, thoughts, and actions. We prioritize God less and emphasize the world more.

This transition may occur gradually as the deceit of the world chokes faith out of us, or it may happen immediately due to a significant event or trauma in life. The cares of this world impacts each believer's life differently but examples include:

- The temporal takes precedence over the eternal.
- We pursue pleasure rather than holiness.
- We seek the approval of men rather than God.
- Our lifestyles mirror the world not Jesus.
- We submit to self rather than Christ.
- We deny the Spirit rather than deny the flesh.

As a result, we fail to primarily focus on God, fulfilling His will, and bringing Him glory. Instead, our lives evidence a passion for the things and cares of the world and we concern ourselves with the "pleasures of life" that "bring no fruit to maturity" (Luke 8:14). This occurs in a number of ways but is especially evident in how we spend our free time when not at work or asleep. We invest our time on many activities that include:

- Television.
- Gaming.
- Shopping.
- Entertainment.
- Gardening.
- Family/Friends.
- Sports.
- Relaxing.
- Pampering ourselves.
- Socializing (online and in person).
- Hobbies.
- Hanging out.
- Cooking.
- Exercise.

None of these activities are intrinsically wrong or an inappropriate use of our time. But when they consume the majority of our time and energy, too little remains to invest in our relationship with the Lord. We have a finite amount of time each day, so the more we spend on the activities of this world the less time we spend pursuing our Savior, strengthening our faith, and developing the attributes of Jesus in our lives. What suffers are those activities that nourish our spirit and mature us as believers such as reading Scripture, prayer, listening to God, serving others, and sharing the gospel.

If honest with ourselves, many of us have allowed the cares of this world to choke the Spirit and make us less fruitful, or even unfruitful, for the Lord. After all, how fruitful can any of us be when spending the vast majority of our time on the cares of the world? As we become increasingly consumed with the world we will always be less interested in our relationship with Jesus. And if we only spend brief periods of time with God, how serious can we really be about that relationship?

Let's reflect on that challenge for a moment because it raises a crucial point. How we invest our free time is a more accurate and candid indicator of the sincerity of our faith than anything we might say. For example, assume each of us has four hours of free time per day (I know some may have more and many will have less but the principle is still the same). Now if we spend all but fifteen minutes each day pursuing activities of the world and invest only those fifteen minutes in our relationship with the Lord, what message does that send about the importance of our faith? If we devote most of our free time around enjoying ourselves, at the expense of becoming more mature in our faith, we reveal the cares of this world of greater value to us than God.

Many of us will protest this argument. We will assert that God is our first priority and we place considerable value in our relationship with Him. Some of us will push back on this line of thought and claim it is too legalistic. But is it? No mention is made of having to spend a specific amount of time on your relationship with God; no assertion that you must read your Bible every day and pray for at least two hours to be a real Christian. Rather, the challenge highlights the tremendous disparity between the amount of time we spend on enjoying the activities of this world and the amount of time we spend on growing our faith. What does that say about our priorities? What does it say about our passion? It says a great deal if we listen.

Imagine a father who each night tells his son he loves him as he tucks the boy into bed. After work each day the dad invests his time in activities that exclude his son: going to the gym, reading, hanging out with the guys one night, washing his car. On weekends he plays a round of golf and watches sports on the television. The only time he spends with his son is when he puts him to bed and tells him how much he loves him. What message does the son learn? He yearns to spend all his time with dad but his dad is too busy doing other things. Does he learn that his dad loves him? Of course not. He learns that he is not a priority in his dad's life. His dad's actions communicate the truth more than his words. What matters to the son is time with his father, not hearing him express words of care.

It would not surprise us if the son were to tell his dad, "Quit saying you love me and show me. I want to spend time with you, learn from you, and become like you." The son rightfully wants to experience his dad's love by sharing life together and not through occasional affirmations. Could you imagine if the father responded, "I told you I love you, now just trust me", or "Don't be so judgmental, I spend a couple minutes with you before you go to sleep each night", or "Requiring I demonstrate my love with my time is a very legalistic perspective." Such statements are ridiculous. We all know in this example that the best barometer of love is time invested, irrespective of what the dad claims. So it is with our faith. We can claim we love God all we want and proclaim that Jesus is Lord. But unless we invest time with Him, pursue a meaningful relationship with Him, and seek to become like Him, the words are worthless.

With that in mind, I encourage you to take inventory of how you invest your free time in a typical week. Use the list on the previous pages to capture the time you invest in each activity. For ease, just use thirty minute increments; ignore anything you do less than that in a week.

The list is not comprehensive, so you may need to assign some of your activities into the general descriptions such as hobbies and hanging out. Try to be as candid as possible with yourself. Once you finish, return back to the next paragraph.

Now think about how much time you spend with the Lord in a typical week. Consider only time that directly develops your faith and draws you closer to Him such as: prayer, reading Scripture, being still in His presence and listening; group Bible studies, ministering to and serving those in need, and worship. Capture that time with God below.

- Relationship with God.

Most of us will discover that the amount of time we invest deepening our relationship with God represents less than half our free time and often not even 10 percent in a typical week. If we focus 90+ percent of our time on the activities of this world and less than 10 percent on God, is it any surprise we are unfruitful? When the cares of the world dominate our life, we barely impact those around us with the kingdom of God.

God challenges us to bear fruit for His kingdom. To do so, we must become better stewards of our most precious commodity: *time.* Consider specific changes you can make in your life to increase the time you spend with the Lord. Here are some examples to get you thinking:

- Watch one fewer television program this week. And then eliminate another program every week for the remainder of the month. By the end of the month you will have eliminated four programs and freed two to four hours a week for the Lord.
- Resist the urge to shop for the next thirty days (except for absolute necessities).
- Stay off the computer one day a week for the next month (except for legitimate work).
- When you exercise, use the time to actively communicate and talk with the Lord.

- Select one night a week to invest entirely in your relationship with the Lord. Whether for an hour or four, spend that evening each week drawing closer to Jesus.
- Spend one lunch a week reading the Bible, whether at work, on campus, or in your home.

Adopt these changes and make them habits. Do not allow one change to satisfy you; make an additional change every month until you get to the point where half of your free time is spent with the Lord rather than on the things of this world. Your faith will undergo a significant change and your life will take on more of the attributes of Jesus as you spend more time with Him. That will motivate you to invest even more time drawing near to Him.

Those who continue investing a disproportionate amount of time on the activities of the world may do so for a reason. Perhaps they have an inauthentic faith. Anyone who makes excuses for avoiding time with Jesus ought to reflect long and hard on whether he genuinely loves the Lord. Justifying our lack of time with Him certainly suggests we have lost our first love. The danger in that is we may be ill-prepared for Jesus' return, which could happen at any moment. He warned, "take heed to yourselves lest your hearts be weighed down with . . . [the] cares of this life and that Day come on you unexpectedly" (Luke 21:34). Jesus knew the "cares of the world" have the ability to distract us so we take our eyes off our relationship with Him. As a result we neither bear fruit for God nor are we prepared for His return.

Notice the eventual outcome for those consumed by this world. Their hearts focus so much on the world that they become weighed down: weighed down with worry and fear; weighed down with expectations; weighed down by the future. More than just unfruitful, they become completely unaware of anything except the cares of this world. No interest in the Lord, no concern for the hurting, no compassion on the persecuted. That diminished interest in God erodes our relationship with Him to the point that His return catches us by surprise. We fail to comprehend the signs of the times. The possibility that Jesus' return could find us unprepared should cause considerable concern. Jesus offers some pointed words for anyone who claims to believe in and follow Him yet is not ready for His second coming.

Using a wedding as a metaphor, Jesus indicates that those not ready for the bridegroom when he enters the wedding hall will be left outside. Afterward, when they arrive, they ask the bridegroom to open the door, and he responds that he does not know them and leaves them outside (see Matthew 25:1-13). Jesus is the bridegroom, the wedding hall is the kingdom of heaven, and those who remain outside are those who said they were Christians but were not, as evidenced by their ill-preparedness. They did not prepare for His coming, nor did they remain awake and alert. They allowed the world to capture their imagination and distract them. They allowed the cares of this world to consume their focus, love, and attention.

This pattern has been repeated throughout time, going back even to the days of Noah. We are told, "For as in the days before the flood, they were eating and drinking, marrying and giving in marriage, until the day that Noah entered the ark, and did not know until the flood came and took them all away" (Matthew 24:38-39). Jesus comments on the culture of Noah's time as a reference. People get caught up with the lures of this world and forget about God. They focus so much on enjoying the activities of this world they completely ignore the world to come. That perspective yielded serious consequences on the people unprepared for the flood in Noah's day. They were swept away by the flood and died. Similarly, anyone caught unprepared for Jesus' return will also perish. He will neither recognize them nor receive them into His kingdom.

How much do you focus on the cares of this world? What does the way you invest your time suggest? Nothing compares in value to spending time with the Lord and developing an increasingly personal relationship with Him. If we believe that, why do we spend so little time pursuing Him? Why do we allow the "cares of this world" to choke the Word from us, making us unfruitful?

1. In what ways are we unfruitful when we allow the cares of this world to consume us?

2. How do the cares of this world impact our faith and relationship with the Lord?

3. Does your life evidence an interest in the cares of this world? What specific changes can you make to eliminate your cares for this world?

Seek first the kingdom of God and His righteousness,
and all these things shall be added to you.

—Matthew 6:33

CHAPTER 15

Blessing or Curse

Numerous passages in Scripture discuss God's desire to bless His people, especially when they obey Him and follow His will. These verses leave little doubt that God blesses His people abundantly when they keep His commands. However, the American church has taken this principle and distorted it so it no longer reflects biblical truth but false teaching. We define blessing in almost exclusively material and temporal terms. Too often we associates God's blessing as:

- Securing a good, well-paying job.
- Avoiding health or medical problems.
- Owning a comfortable home.
- The absence of stress in life.
- Earning enough income to enjoy a leisurely life.
- Experiencing little difficulty and confronting few trials.
- Owning the latest electronic items such as an iPad, e-reader, or iPhone.
- Feeling happily in control of everything.
- Enjoying the freedom to shop for our desires.
- Appreciating a life of comfort and ease.

But Jesus never defined blessing this way. He viewed a closer relationship with the Father as the ultimate blessing. Experiencing spiritual growth was the reward for submitting to Him as Lord, not growth of your investment portfolio. By defining blessing in material terms rather than as an increase in spiritual maturity, we deceive ourselves.

Jesus said, "For where you treasure is, there your heart will be also" (Matthew 6:21). God wants our treasure in Him, not in material things that pass away. Why then would He "bless" us with innumerable things that have a destructive impact on our faith by competing with Him for our love? Why would He "bless" us with stuff that leads us away from Him in the use of our time and talents? Jesus knows we have need for food and clothing, and He provides those necessities (see Matthew 6:25-34). He never suggests He will provide us with luxury or excess beyond our needs. He never indicates He will provide things we desire from our lustful hearts.

Nevertheless, most of us have determined that God loves us so much He wants us happy and will give us whatever we desire to facilitate our happiness. We tend to believe God wants us to own more and more material things, which are newer, nicer, and better than what we currently have. Essentially, He lives to give us the desires of our heart, and our hearts desire the things of this world.

Sadly, we hold this belief so strongly we fail to realize that often our increased possessions do not represent blessings from God but curses from Satan. Now before you get all fired-up and start yelling unpleasant remarks, reflect on that for a minute. The "blessings" we claim God provides frequently represent false idols for many of us. Our love and frenetic pursuit of worldly things and the pleasures of this world have reached the point that it constitutes a form of worship.

That dedication to acquiring stuff, though, has come at a cost to our faith. Pursuing Jesus and the things of heaven no longer consumes us. Faith is not our first priority and Jesus is no longer our first love. (See Revelation 2:4.) So why would God "bless" us with the things of this world that eventually separate us from Him? Why would He gift us with benefits that weaken and sometimes even destroy our relationship with Him? Why would He decide making us happy in this world is of more value than making us more like His Son in preparation for the next? Why would He heap on us stuff that risks fueling sin in our lives? Why would He reward us with items that threaten to become false idols? Why would He give us material things in response to our spiritual growth, and risk undoing all our spiritual maturity? The answers, of course, are that He would not do any of those things. Our confusion lies in our distorted view of blessing.

We must realize that material things often represent temptation from Satan to lure us away from the Lord. Satan knows that fancy things lead many believers further from their relationship with Jesus and make them increasingly ineffective. Moreover, if he can affirm in them the idea that material things represent a blessing from God for a job well done, then getting believers to fall prey to the trap is easy. Satan has destroyed untold multitudes by "blessing" them with the riches of this world, and telling them they are from God. And because so many of us desire these material blessings, we readily buy-in to the lie.

When we obey, follow, and serve God, He indeed wants to bless us. However, that blessing takes on primarily a spiritual component rather than a temporal one. Paul tells us "the God and Father of our Lord Jesus Christ . . . has blessed us with every spiritual blessing" (Ephesians 1:3). God has already provided us with so many spiritual blessings including forgiveness, mercy, faith, a tender heart for others, salvation, and His Spirit. Unfortunately, many of us fail to reflect on these blessings and rarely express gratitude to God for giving them to us. Why do we struggle so much with the idea that God's blessings generally are spiritual? I suspect it is because our flesh defines blessing for us, and it lusts for the things of this world.

That raises an interesting question. If we define blessing in material terms because our flesh persuades us to think this way, how spiritually mature are we? How much have we really grown in the faith if we continue to take our cues from our sin nature? And if we are not as mature spiritually as we thought, then perhaps there is no reason for God to bless us for our obedience and faith. In other words, material "blessings" may actually reflect spiritual stagnation or decline, not spiritual maturity and growth. If we possess a truly mature faith, we would want our blessing in spiritual terms; those gifts from God that spur further spiritual growth. We would have little interest in worldly "blessings" because of the risk they set us back in our walk with the Lord. The blessings we would desire from the Lord would include:

- Humility
- Mercy
- A gentle spirit
- Holiness
- Generosity
- Hunger for His Word
- Boldness in faith
- Kindness
- Sacrificial living
- Heart for missions
- Love for the "least of these"
- Selflessness

Jesus said, "Seek first the kingdom of God and His righteousness, and all these things shall be added to you" (Matthew 6:33). So what does "all these things" represent, that God will give us. It represents spiritual gifts like the list above. How do we know that? Because Jesus does not give us these gifts unless we seek His kingdom first, as well as His righteousness. What does it mean to seek the kingdom of God? It includes placing His will above ours, seeking His attributes and adopting His passions.

Now when we seek first His kingdom we acquire a different perspective on what "these things" means. We recognize that it primarily represents spiritual benefits rather than temporal ones. Moreover, we redefine the material component in more limited terms. We understand it represents our needs only, and not our lusts or desires. This modified definition of blessing does not bother us because we are seeking His kingdom first anyhow. We find satisfaction in having only our needs met; we are neither bitter nor disappointed that our desires go unmet. In fact, we rejoice that they remain unfulfilled because we are aware they lead us from the Lord. Our pursuit of the kingdom first has transformed our priorities in how we want God to bless us.

QUESTIONS:

1. How has seeking the kingdom of God first impacted your life?

2. If you place the Lord first, will that affect how you define His blessings?

3. Jesus observed, "where you treasure is, there your heart will be also." Where is your treasure?

PART IV

Difficult because: We Must Evidence Faith

We have invested considerable time discussing the importance of living faith in substance, especially as it relates to dying to self and refusing to love the things of this world. We continue the theme of what authentic faith looks like in the life of a believer. In the next three chapters we explore that subject in the following areas:

1. Avoiding a pattern of sin
2. Persevering in faith.
3. Living faith in action not words

Applying Jesus' lessons in these areas continues our discussion around the difficult path a believer follows. We learn that genuine faith does not tolerate a pattern of sin. Believers will sin but they seek the presence of the Holy Spirit to resist and overcome it. We learn that sincere faith endures. It does not last for a season and then burn-out or return to a life of iniquity. Finally, we learn that faith is revealed in action, if real, and not in words. In each area God's power equips the believer to achieve victory over sin, sustain his faith, and live obedience in his conduct.

Do you not know that the unrighteous will not inherit
the kingdom of God? Do not be deceived.

—1 Corinthians 6:9

CHAPTER 16

Avoid Practicing Sin

God calls us to a life of holiness upon professing faith in Jesus. While we never become perfect on Earth, God expects us to leave our lifestyle of sin. We must renounce whatever sins we practiced prior to accepting Christ and pursue lives that reflect a pattern of increased holiness and decreased sinfulness. We sin less frequently, less broadly, and no longer willfully pursue a sinful lifestyle.

Let's explore God's Word regarding the incompatibility between a lifestyle of sin and the life of a believer. Near the end of his epistle to the church at Galatia, Paul lists a number of works that reflect a life lived in the flesh. They include: adultery, licentiousness, idolatry, sorcery, hatred, contentions, jealousies, outbursts of wrath, selfish ambitions, heresies, envy, murders, drunkenness, and revelries, among others (Galatians 5:19-20). With respect to those behaviors, Paul asserts, "those who practice such things will *not* inherit the kingdom of God" (Galatians 5:21, emphasis added). Paul has argued throughout this epistle that faith represents a gift of God that flows from His mercy. Yet he now concludes his message to the Galatian church by emphasizing that those who practice the works of the flesh will not inherit the kingdom of God.

- They do not have salvation.
- They will not spend eternity with Jesus.
- They will not receive God's grace.
- They were never born again.

So how do we reconcile these two positions? How can Paul claim salvation comes by grace alone yet at the same time declare that those who practice the works of the flesh have no salvation? He asserts both because both are true. Sincerity of faith represents the determining variable. Anyone who genuinely accepts Jesus as Savior and earnestly submits to Him as Lord no longer practices the works of the flesh.

Will a believer still stumble and sin in the areas Paul mentions? Yes. But those acts of sin will decrease in frequency. He will conduct himself with increased holiness in each area. His habits will mirror the Lord's behavior more and more as he resists practicing a lifestyle of sin. He does not "play with" sin, nor does he visit a particular sin throughout the week. He refuses to dabble in the works of the flesh. When he stumbles his spirit grieves because he knows his conduct grieves the Holy Spirit. Moreover, when he sins he goes to God in prayer and immediately repents. So while a Christian certainly sins, he refuses to pursue a lifestyle of sin. Do you currently practice any works of the flesh? Does your life reflect a pattern of sin? If so, repent immediately, ask the Lord forgiveness, and stop pursuing those acts of sin.

- Stop the adulterous relationship.
- Stop deceitful business practices.
- Stop looking at Internet porn.
- Stop participating in the occult.
- Stop getting drunk.
- Stop imagining lustful thoughts.
- Stop shopping for things you desire.
- Stop believing the heresies of the apostate church.
- Stop envying others and their lives.
- Stop your selfish ambitions—for your career, reputation, and wealth.
- Stop lashing out in anger.
- Stop pursuing worldly decadence.
- Stop your idolatrous love for anything but God.
- Stop hating the person who wronged you.
- Stop embracing the bitterness that consumes you.

How do you quit practicing the works of the flesh that devour you? How do you stop pursuing whatever pattern of sin imprisons you? You submit to the leadership of the Holy Spirit. No one conquers sin on their own strength. The holiest believer who fights sin on his own strength will always lose. Maybe not the first time he is tempted, maybe not the hundredth time, but eventually he succumbs to sin if he relies on himself to conquer sin.

Defeating sin requires awareness that it is part of a larger spiritual battle for souls. "For we do not wrestle against flesh and blood, but against principalities, against powers, against the rulers of the darkness of this age, against spiritual hosts of wickedness in the heavenly places" (Ephesians 6:12). Sin represents a spiritual condition and must be addressed in spiritual terms. Sin eventually overcomes any effort you make by yourself because the spiritual forces fighting you will increase in number and intensity until they can defeat you (see Luke 11:24-26). Triumph over sin only occurs through the Holy Spirit. Scripture informs us, "Not by might nor by power, but by My Spirit" (Zechariah 4:6). Only the Holy Spirit gives us victory over sin because only He can defeat the unseen spiritual forces behind the temptation.

I recall struggling with a sin for a number of years. I kept trying to defeat it by sheer resistance. When tempted, I would "will" myself not to sin and insist I would not stumble. But I always did. I had periods of success, only to fall back into the sinful habit. Eventually I succeeded in avoiding the sin for a number of months and began to think, "This is easy. As long as I try really hard to avoid sin, I can keep it at bay. The only reason anyone remains in sin is because he is not serious enough about stopping the sin in his life." What an arrogant perspective I had. Predictably, a couple days later I had fallen back into my sin. You see, I had relied on my own strength to defeat sin. And when I met with a modest amount of success, I credited myself for overcoming sin. In doing so I developed spiritual pride in my heart and confidence in my own abilities to defeat spiritual forces. That recipe always leads to failure because it is grounded in self and breeds arrogance. Refraining from the sin today is due entirely to the power of the Holy Spirit.

His presence provides us day to day victory over sin. Does that mean we sit back, relax, and allow Him to do all the work of removing sin in our lives? Absolutely not. God calls us to "take up the whole armor of God, that you may be able to withstand in the evil day, and having done all, to stand" (Ephesians 6:13). He calls us to action. The armor of God represents our weapons of warfare against sin and the forces of darkness and includes: truth, righteousness, peace, faith, salvation, and God's Word. These are the weapons of God we use in battle. Through them God equips us to fight the spiritual battle. Combined with "prayer and supplication in the Spirit" we are able to remain "watchful to this end with all perseverance" (Ephesians 6:18). While Jesus gives us the victory He does not expect as to stand around as passive participants in this warfare. As good soldiers of the Lord we are to actively fight—study the Bible, live godly, share truth, and pray.

We must also be diligent and resilient in the battle. "Be self-controlled, be vigilant; because your adversary the devil walks about like a roaring lion, seeking whom he may devour. Resist him, steadfast in the faith" (1 Peter 5:8-9). Peter informs us that our enemy is a predator and always looking to destroy God's people. When he attacks with enticement, we must resist and exercise self-control. Although God calls us to fight temptation and the spiritual forces, we must recognize that victory comes from Him. "Therefore submit to God. Resist the devil and he will flee from you. Draw near to God and He will draw near to you" (James 4:7-8). The devil flees from us when we resist, but only when we submit to God first. He empowers us to both resist and repel Satan, but we must draw near to Him. If you fail, do not give up. He is faithful to forgive you and restore you. But you must continue to fight, avoid sinful situations and resist. And remember to give Him glory when He does give you victory over sin.

He who willfully pursues sins of the flesh does not inherit the kingdom; he falls short because his actions reveal the true nature of his heart. He never genuinely trusted Jesus nor believed with all his heart, soul, mind, and strength. His actions demonstrate that a passion for sin resides in his heart rather than a love for the Spirit.

John illuminates the distinction in his first epistle. "If we say that we have fellowship with Him, and walk in darkness, we lie and do not practice the truth. But if we walk in the light as He is in the light, we have fellowship with one another, and the blood of Jesus Christ His Son cleanses us from all sin" (1 John 1:6-7). In both instances sin occurs. However, the one who walks in darkness deceives himself and has an insincere faith. He enjoys no fellowship with the Lord because he practices a lifestyle of sin marked by the darkness.

In contrast, the one who walks in the light walks with the Lord. He develops habits of godliness and seeks to obey Jesus in all ways. When he stumbles and sins, the blood of Jesus cleanses him before God. The pattern of behavior distinguishes the one in darkness and the one in light. Ongoing sin, a lifestyle of the flesh, and habits of wickedness mark the man who walks in darkness; he does not know the Lord. Growth in godliness, a lifestyle in the Spirit, and a pattern of obedience mark the man who walks in the light. He still sins, but neither practices nor pursues it as a lifestyle. "For God did not call us to uncleanness, but in holiness" (1 Thessalonians 4:7).

Paul reinforces this point in his epistle to the church at Corinth. "Do you not know that the unrighteous will not inherit the kingdom of God? Do not be deceived" (1 Corinthians 6:9). Jesus' blood covers the sin of the believer so he appears righteous before God. Without the blood of Christ covering our iniquities, we face judgment for our unrighteousness. Paul's point to the Corinthians is that those living in sin are unrighteous before God because they do not have Christ. Righteousness comes from Jesus as a product of genuine faith in Him, which leads to forsaking all patterns of abominable conduct.

You may appear holy to others; the Pharisees did as well. You may claim to love God and serve Him, as did the Pharisees two thousand years ago. And what did the Lord say to the Pharisees? He chastised them for having an appearance of godliness but remaining wicked, self-focused, and far from God in their hearts. He exclaimed, "Even so you also outwardly appear righteous to men, but inside you are full of hypocrisy and lawlessness" (Matthew 23:28).

Do not think because your friends, family, and pastor vouch for your spiritual health that you therefore have genuine faith. Does their support validate your faith? It most certainly does not. If you practice the works of the flesh, you possess an artificial faith. You are a modern-day Pharisee who appears righteous to men, but inside you are full of selfishness and wickedness. Your faith no more gets you into heaven than did the faith of the Pharisees.

Paul brings to a conclusion this message that salvation flows from God's grace but reflects a repudiation of the works of the flesh. He warns us not to let the world mislead us. "Do not be deceived. God is not mocked; for whatever a man sows, that he will also reap. For he who sows to his flesh will of the flesh reap corruption, but he who sows to the Spirit will of the Spirit reap everlasting life" (Galatians 6:7-8).

God is not fooled. Regardless of what you claim, your actions reveal your true belief. At the end times, when the Lord returns, He will "bring to light the hidden things of darkness and reveal the counsels of the hearts" (1 Corinthians 4:5). If you currently practice any work of the flesh, then God will judge you and you will reap eternal death. Make no mistake. It is not enough to simply affirm acceptance of salvation through Jesus. Paul insists that a believer reflect his commitment to Jesus in refusing to follow a pattern of sin. Earnestly examine your life as to whether there exists any ongoing commitment to a particular sin. If so, repent immediately and quit practicing that sin.

QUESTIONS:

1. Although a believer continues to sin, Paul says no one who practices sinful behavior will inherit the kingdom. What is the distinction?

2. Is there an area of your life where you practice sin or pursue a sinful lifestyle?

3. What action will you take to stop this practice?

Therefore, my beloved brethren, be steadfast, immovable, always abounding in the work of the Lord, knowing that your labor is not in vain in the Lord.

—1 Corinthians 15:58

CHAPTER 17

Persevere in Faith

Persevering in the faith can be challenging at times. Distractions from the world can consume you. Troubles in your personal life can discourage you. Painful experiences can disillusion and confuse you, especially when they create unanswered questions. Temptations can return you to a sinful lifestyle. Persecution can drive you from the faith. Remaining steadfast in faith throughout life and growing more mature in your relationship with Jesus is no easy task.

It is insufficient to claim faith in Christ for a season and then fall back into a lifestyle of sin. God calls us to persevere in faith through whatever challenges and difficulties arise. Anyone who fails to remain steadfast in his faith until the end demonstrates a lack of commitment. His faith has a foundation of sand that cannot withstand the storms of life Satan throws at him. His inability to persevere reveals an absence of authentic faith.

Anyone sincerely committed to the Lord perseveres through all challenges he faces. God equips each believer with the power of the Holy Spirit to remain steadfast in faith no matter the circumstance, irrespective of the cost, and regardless the consequence. We need to recognize that challenges or difficulties in life often represent a spiritual attack from the devil to destroy our faith. To persevere, we must focus on fulfilling God's will and remain mindful of His warning that we remain prepared for His return.

Difficulties or discouragement are not the only challenges to remaining faithful. Often, success proves far more disruptive to our relationship with the Lord than the hard times. Success tends to distract us from God by providing us reputations to protect, careers to maintain, and pleasures to pursue. Too often these worldly benefits enslave us, leading us from the faith. Moreover, when the world threatens to take these away due to our faith, it can become easy to compromise. Many sell out their faith in order to remain ensconced in the lifestyle they love, and find it easier to compromise their beliefs than forego the world's enticements. Such individuals should consider Paul's admonition to the church at Colossae first, before embarking down the road of compromised and abandoned faith.

"And you, who once were alienated and enemies in your mind by wicked works, yet now He has reconciled in the body of His flesh through death, to present you holy, and blameless, and irreproachable in His sight—if indeed you continue in the faith grounded and steadfast, and are not moved away from the hope of the gospel which you heard, which was preached to every creature under heaven" (Colossians 1:21-23).

Paul recounts the historical condition of the believer before Christ, and the transformation that occurs subsequent to committing his life to Jesus. He was steeped in wicked behavior and his thoughts were consumed with depravity, which left him an enemy of God. But the suffering death of Jesus atones for the believer's sin so he is reconciled to God. Moreover, His shed blood covers our sin so God sees us as holy and blameless saints rather than the wretched sinners we are. Paul then qualifies our appearance before God as righteous and without fault; it only occurs if we remain steadfast in faith.

If we move away from our faith in Jesus, no such substitution occurs. When we choose to return to a lifestyle of sin and selfishness, God does not view our souls through the prism of Jesus' blood but sees only our wickedness. Paul asserts that Jesus' presentation of us to the Father as holy and blameless occurs *if* we continue in the faith and do not depart from the gospel we have heard and received. Some may respond that the "perseverance of the saints" precludes losing salvation. That is true. The Holy Spirit keeps those to whom He has been entrusted. The inability to persevere does not cause the loss of salvation; rather, it demonstrates the absence of salvation from the beginning. In that sense, I would modify the well-known axiom "Once saved, always saved" to instead affirm, "*If* saved, always saved."

Jesus verifies this position. In the parable of the sower He remarks that some will endure "only for a time" because "when tribulation or persecution arises for the word's sake, immediately they stumble" (Mark 4:17). They do not persevere because they are not rooted in Jesus. Note that such individuals initially receive the gospel with gladness. They happily embrace the gospel and immediately profess faith in Christ. However, they do not remain committed. Whether their profession was an emotional response in the moment or they entered into faith with the wrong motivation or they simply failed to count the cost is unclear. What is clear, though, is that they fail to endure. As soon as difficulty occurs or they face persecution, they stumble. They turn from the faith they so readily embraced. They bear no fruit nor evidence the sustaining power of the Holy Spirit.

In describing the difficulties that await believers in the end days, Jesus informs His disciples, "But he who endures to the end shall be saved" (Mark 13:13). He clarifies that those who experience a momentary faith have no salvation. Jesus offers a simple but clear message: Genuine faith endures until the end. John reinforces this in his first epistle: "For whatever is born of God overcomes the world. And this is the victory that has overcome the world—our faith" (1 John 5:4).

Similarly, Jesus counsels each of the seven churches in Revelation 2-3 to overcome in order to sit with Him in heaven. For five of the churches, that means repenting of an identified sin (or sins) and remaining faithful in those areas in which they excel. For the faithful and persecuted churches, it means remaining faithful in death and persevering through the trials to come. In all instances, though, we must hold firm the gospel of Jesus and maintain faith no matter the cost.

As believers, we must endure and continue in our commitment to the Lord. Do not be overcome by the world. Do not fall back into those sins which easily ensnare you. Do not allow hardship to deter you from finishing the race. Eternity with God far outweighs the momentary pleasure and satisfaction enjoyed if you backslide. Be encouraged that the Holy Spirit sustains every believer who commits himself to the Lord.

1. Why do some who claim faith in Jesus eventually return to a lifestyle of sin?

2. Why does God call us to persevere in our faith? What does that demonstrate?

3. What preventive measures can you take to avoid falling back into your old ways?

So they come to you as people do, they sit before you as My people, and they hear your words, but they do not do them; for with their mouth they show much love, but their hearts pursue their own gain. Indeed you are to them as a very lovely song of one who has a pleasant voice and can play well on an instrument; for they hear your words, but they do not do them. And when this comes to pass—surely it will come—then they will know that a prophet has been among them.

—Ezekiel 33:31-33

CHAPTER 18

Live Faith

Jesus wants His followers to live a life consistent with His teachings and expects them to keep His commands no matter how difficult. He desires a substantive relationship with every person who claims to follow Him as a disciple. Jesus has no interest in lip service; He finds no pleasure in people who obey with their words but whose actions demonstrate a heart far from Him.

Professing faith in Jesus and claiming to love Him presents little difficulty for most Americans. Our culture is rooted in the Christian faith, so giving Him honor with our lips requires no real challenge. The difficult part is living out the life of faith Jesus calls us to live. Substantively obeying His commands requires a more focused and sincere faith. As we learned in earlier chapters, Jesus' requirements for His disciples run counter to our sinful ways.

Since the beginning of time man has struggled with this challenge of living faith in action and not merely honoring God in words only. The Israelites struggled with the same issue thousands of years ago. Their faith emphasized appearance rather than substance. They spoke favorably of God and His prophet but did not translate those words into action. Instead they pursued a path of rebellion while honoring God with their lips. As a result of the abominations they committed, the Lord informs them they will not inhabit the land they desired to possess (see Ezekiel 33:23-29). Their behavior had consequences. God does not bless a people who live inconsistent with His commands.

Curiously, their depraved conduct occurred despite Ezekiel regularly preaching the word of God to them. He shared what God expected of them and the plans He had for them. Moreover, the Israelites expressed genuine interest in hearing God's message. They encouraged each other and their neighbors to come and listen to God's Word as told through His messenger, Ezekiel. "They speak to one another, everyone saying to his brother, 'Please come and hear what the word is that comes from the Lord'" (Ezekiel 33:30). The Israelites recognized that Ezekiel spoke for the Lord. They expressed enthusiasm for listening to those words and made an effort to get others to hear Ezekiel's preaching, which came from God Himself. The Israelites were neither ashamed of God nor disinterested in hearing what He had to say.

Similarly, many Americans express an interest in hearing the word of God and the message their pastor shares each week about God's truth. As with the Israelites, many actively bring others to church and encourage them to come and hear what God has to say through His servant. However, attending church, listening to and even enjoying the pastor's messages, and inviting others to church means nothing if our faith stops there. The Israelites were doing as much; they loved listening to God's message but refused to allow that message to change their hearts. They embraced God's Word with their ears but failed to apply God's Word with their lives.

That failure precluded them from having a genuine, healthy relationship with God. That disconnect resulted in the Israelites committing all kinds of abominations against the Lord because their hearts were distant from Him. They were desensitized to His commands and His will. Consequently, they developed a lifestyle of sin despite their excitement for God's Word and hearing it regularly. That wicked behavior and lifestyle eventually led to God's judgment.

It is important we understand that the Israelites enjoyed assembling and hearing God's truth yet simply refused to follow His truth: "they hear [God's] words, but they do not do them" (Ezekiel 33:31b). Do you see that listening to God's Word was not enough; going to church regularly and taking notes during the sermon has no value unless it translates into obedience to God's Word. Unless we apply to our lives what the pastor teaches, God is not pleased. He wants us to live His words and truth, not simply understand and appreciate them. Otherwise, we make the same mistake the Israelites made.

In fact, the Israelites did more than just assemble to hear God's Word from the prophet Ezekiel. They actually praised God with their lips and told the prophet they enjoyed his message. We are told "with their mouth they show much love" (Ezekiel 33:31b). One would have thought they were very close to the Lord since they said the right things, expressed a love for God and others, and showed enthusiasm for learning what God had to say. Too often our faith mirrors the Israelites. It is robust in its outward appearance and impresses others, but it never takes root in the heart; it never leads to repentance and a transformed life.

Their problem was they disobeyed the truths they learned. They held an intellectual interest in God and His word, and that served as a social bond among the Israelites. However, they declined to set aside their selfish ways and subject themselves to God's commands. Ezekiel tells us that although their mouths showed much love, "their hearts pursue their own gain." Despite listening to God's word on a regular basis, the Israelites demonstrated no change in their lives. They continued to live for themselves. They had a faith that honored God with their lips but their hearts remained unaffected. God makes clear He considers such behavior unacceptable. He loathes the practice of professing love for Him but refusing to follow His Word.

For the American church, we must carefully consider this lesson. As a collective church body it seems obvious we mirror too closely the example of the Israelites. Too many of us attend church regularly and listen intently to the pastor preach, but our lives display almost no impact. We do not exhibit changed priorities from a vibrant and real faith. Instead, like the Israelites, our hearts remain committed to pursuing abominable conduct. Similarly, we love to tell the pastor how great his message is and how we were moved by his words, but "we do not do them" (Ezekiel 33:32). Selfish motivations likely drive many of those who live inconsistent lives, "who suppose that godliness is a means of gain" (1 Timothy 6:5b). Not true godliness of course, but the appearance thereof. We must avoid the same mistake the Israelites made in how they practiced faith. We must live God's truths.

James warned the early church about this issue as well. He encouraged believers to "lay aside all filthiness and overflow of wickedness, and receive with meekness the implanted word, which is able to save your souls. But be doers of the word, and not hearers only, deceiving yourselves" (James 1:21-22). James makes it clear that rejecting our lifestyle of wickedness accompanies our receipt of God's Word. We cannot embrace God's Word in a meaningful way and continue our pursuit of sinful behavior. That was the error the Israelites made, deceiving themselves. Similarly, we deceive ourselves if we do not implement God's truth and obey His commands in our day-to-day lives.

Paul also observed such insincere followers in the first-century church. He describes them as those who "profess to know God but in works they deny Him, being abominable, disobedient, and disqualified for every good work" (Titus 1:16). Such Christians talk a good game. But as the old maxim goes, "talk is cheap." Paul sheds light on the motivations of these faux believers, explaining that the basis of their faith is the pursuit of "dishonest gain" (Titus 1:11). They claim a Christian faith because they believe they can achieve their selfish objectives more easily. They remain in love with the world and its treasures and use Christianity as a cover to fulfill their lusts. They "talk the talk" but fail to "walk the walk."

As a result of their disobedience: they are "disqualified for every good work" (Titus 1:16). What are the good works from which pseudo believers are disqualified? Paul explains that Jesus "redeem[ed] us from every lawless deed and [purified] for Himself His own special people, zealous for good works" (Titus 2:14). The good works are opportunities the Lord has provided for His followers to commit. They do so with zeal and joy, not out of obligation or a begrudging spirit. An individual disqualified from such works cannot perform them. He cannot glorify God in such actions because he does not obey Christ. His heart yearns to disobey the Lord, and therefore Jesus does not allow such a person to commit good works. He is disqualified from them.

God created us for these good works, and His grace saves us that we might commit them. Paul tells the church at Ephesus that we are "created in Christ Jesus for good works, which God prepared beforehand that we should walk in them" (Ephesians 2:10). We exist not for ourselves but for Him and the commission of good works on His behalf.

Regarding faux followers of God, Asaph remarks, "The haters of the Lord would pretend submission to Him, but their fate would endure forever" (Psalm 81:15). He labels as "hater of God" all those who honor God with their lips alone but whose hearts are far from Him. That is strong language. Asaph indicates that anyone who says they love God but refuses to substantively submit to Him, actually hates Him. He only pretends to love God. Imagine the level of deceit involved for someone to believe they love God, but in reality they hate Him. God's Word tells us that is the case for anyone whose love is manifested in words only. Asaph informs us that the ultimate fate for such individuals endures forever. They experience eternity separated from the Lord.

The same fate awaits each of us if we limit our faith to mere words. We must avoid the human tendency to "glory in appearance and not in heart" (2 Corinthians 5:12b). Such inconsistency reflects a disingenuous faith mired in deceit. Each of us should examine his life and ensure no such inconsistency exists. Confirm that your faith reflects obedience to the Lord in substance and not in words alone. "Let us not love in word or in tongue, but in deed and in truth" (1 John 3:18).

============================= QUESTIONS: =============================

1. How do you apply God's truth and commands and not just verbally agree with them?

2. Why does God want us to live our faith in action rather than just offer Him lip service?

3. Can you identify an area in your life in which you honor God with your words but your heart remains disobedient and rebellious? What will you do to address that sin?

PART V

Difficult because: We Must Put Others First

U p to this point, the difficulties in living as Jesus' disciples have involved our relationship with the Lord and our ongoing battle with sin. Now we explore our relationship with others and what the "difficult path" looks like as we pursue those relationships. Jesus had much to say about how He expects His disciples to treat others. He challenges us to love others even when they treat us with hate and disrespect. He encourages us to adopt a posture of humility in serving others. He requires we forgive others when they wrong us, no matter how often or how severe. He sends us into the world as His ambassadors to testify of His love, mercy and salvation. He expects us to correct each other when one falls into a lifestyle of iniquity. He wants us to pray for others and their needs before we petition Him for our own.

Forgiveness. Humility. Love. These three attributes do not always come easy. They are difficult to implement when responding to people who hurt us or treat us with contempt, disrespect, or hate. Additionally, sharing our faith with others, correcting those in error, and praying sacrificially are actions we do not pursue naturally. But Jesus requires we make them our habits in how we interact with others. He provided an example in each area; He does not ask us to behave differently than He did toward others. We ought to model ourselves and our conduct after His example. In following His example, we draw people to Him. They will observe the contrasting conduct between how a believer treats others and how the world treats others, especially strangers, the marginalized, and those who mistreat or despise us.

We discuss each of these behavioral attributes in the next six chapters and study the example Jesus provided in establishing the difficult path to follow as His disciples.

You have heard that it was said, "You shall love your neighbor and hate your enemy." But I say to you, love your enemies, bless those who curse you, do good to those who hate you, and pray for those who spitefully use you and persecute you, that you may be sons of your Father in heaven; for He makes His sun rise on the evil and on the good, and sends rain on the just and on the unjust. For if you love those who love you, what reward have you? Do not even the tax collectors do the same? And if you greet your brethren only, what do you do more than others? Do not even the tax collectors do so? Therefore you shall be perfect, just as your Father in heaven is perfect.

—Matthew 5:43-48

CHAPTER 19

Love

Who do you love? No doubt you love members of your family. Probably you love your closest friends as well. But most of us would likely hesitate to say we love anyone beyond our family and close personal friends. We typically reserve our deepest love for those with whom we have a familial bond or have developed an emotional intimacy.

Now reflect on how you demonstrate love for them. Surely you tell them, "I love you," with some regularity. Likely you express an interest in their thoughts and feelings and show them acts of kindness. You share your views and dreams with them, making yourself emotionally vulnerable, revealing the trust you have in them. You invest time with them and express happiness over sharing special moments together. Certainly we all want to treat our loved ones so well all the time.

But have you ever behaved poorly toward a loved one? Have you done something to a loved one for which you had to ask forgiveness? Have you ever disrespected a loved one or said something hurtful? Ever made a loved one feel worthless, discouraged, or ashamed? Ever harmed a loved one emotionally? Most of us have said or done something we later regretted because it did not show love. If we are honest, we probably say or do such things more frequently than we care to admit.

On reflection, I have discovered my unloving behavior generally stems from one source: selfishness. I have been wronged and respond back in kind. I did not get my way, so I say or do something to express my displeasure. I am in a bad mood and direct that frustration against a loved one. It saddens me that my love for self sometimes leads me to treat loved ones in an unloving way. Whenever I focus on myself, I risk treating someone I love as if I cared very little about them. I have learned that loving others requires I put aside that love for self and esteem loved ones of greater importance than myself. I must hold their interests in higher regard than my own and put their needs ahead of mine.

While such adjustments improve how I treat loved ones, it is not always easy to consistently behave that way. I suspect we all find it difficult at times to put the interests of loved ones ahead of our own. It can be a challenge to always prioritize their needs higher than ours. Responding in love when we perceive ourselves to have suffered a wrong can prove difficult. But true love compels us to conduct ourselves in such a way. While demonstrating love to family and close friends can pose a challenge in some circumstances, we do so because we genuinely love them.

As Christians, we are compelled to love everyone, even those outside our circle of emotional intimacy. Beyond family and close friends, Jesus calls us to love our neighbors, our work colleagues, and even complete strangers. The love He calls us to share with others is not passive or casual. It is not a lesser love than what we reserve for family and friends. It is a love that sacrifices. While we find it considerably more difficult to show such love to those we barely know or to complete strangers, that is exactly the love Jesus calls us to demonstrate to them. Recall Jesus' parable of the Samaritan.

> A certain man went down from Jerusalem to Jericho, and fell among thieves, who stripped him of his clothing, wounded him, and departed, leaving him half dead. Now by chance a certain priest came down that road. And when he saw him, he passed on the other side. Likewise a Levite, when he arrived at the place, came and looked, and passed by on the other side. But a certain Samaritan, as he journeyed, came where he was.

And when he saw him, he had compassion on him, and went
to him and bandaged his wounds, pouring on oil and wine,
and he set him on his own animal, brought him to an inn,
and took care of him. On the next day, when he departed, he
took out two denarii, gave them to the innkeeper, and said to
him, "Take care of him, and whatever more you spend, when
I come again, I will repay you." (Luke 10:30-35)

The Samaritan exemplified the love of Christ in several ways.

First, he had compassion for another, a less fortunate stranger. He
genuinely cared about the well-being of this stranger. His initial reaction
to the man was empathy. Different from pity, empathy takes action
whereas pity merely expresses brief sorrow and then moves on without
helping. Compassion compelled the Samaritan to help the stranger. The
Samaritan saw the humanity of the stranger, and as a child of God. He
saw him as having value and worthy of kindness and care.

Second, the Samaritan took action. He assisted the stranger in
a substantive way. In personally bandaging the man's wounds, the
Samaritan treated the stranger as family. Moreover, he sought to comfort
the stranger from his pain by pouring oil and wine on his wounds. He
made an effort to begin the healing process for this man; healing his
physical wounds with the oil and healing his emotional wounds by
displaying love. This behavior represents the mindset Christ wants us
to hold in showing His love. Treat every person with the love we show
our closest family or friend.

Third, the Samaritan set aside his own agenda to meet a need. He
sacrificed whatever plans he had for that day to take care of the stranger.
No doubt he had a list of errands and tasks he hoped to accomplish that
day. He had other priorities when he left his house that morning but he
put those aside when he saw a fellow man in need. He acted sacrificially.
He denied his own interests to show love to someone he had never met.
He took a full day out of his schedule to assist a needy stranger.

As Jesus sacrificed for us, He calls us to sacrifice for others, daily.
God puts in our path strangers and He expects us to adjust our priorities

to meet their needs. He expects us to deny our own interests to meet their interests, and in doing so demonstrate His love to an unloving world.

Fourth, the Samaritan demonstrated generosity. He gave the innkeeper money to care for the stranger until he returned to health, and guaranteed to recompense him for any additional costs he incurred. Love does not stop at the wallet. It compels us to use our resources to help others.

In these ways the Samaritan displayed love substantively. He did not confine his love to words, telling the stranger, "God bless you," as he hurried past. His refused to define his love in spiritual terms, offering to pray that God would restore the man to health quickly. His love was not from afar, simply calling 911 and asking someone else to come and help. Instead, the Samaritan lived his love in action. He touched, he comforted, he healed, and he invested his time and money. Unlike his religious peers (the priest and the Levite), the Samaritan demonstrated genuine love—the love Jesus wants us to show others.

Jesus commands His disciples to display His love to everyone, especially strangers. His love differs dramatically from the worlds. His love shows compassion and takes action. His love sacrifices and requires we deny ourselves. His love is generous. While such love may seem impossible to give strangers, that is exactly whom Jesus calls us to love as His ambassadors to the world. His parable clearly makes that point. It is insufficient to simply love those who love us.

As if loving strangers substantively and sacrificially were not enough, Jesus takes it a step further. He establishes a new standard. He requires we show love to those who hate us, and respond with kindness and compassion when ill treated by our enemies. Anyone who claims Him as Lord, Jesus informs, must love those who spitefully use them and who treat them with contempt. As His followers we must conduct ourselves with a love that captures the world's attention, a love that easily identifies Christians from those of other faiths. Such behavior sharply contrasts the love of Jesus and the love of the world. By loving our enemies, believers provide the world a glimpse into the loving, forgiving, and caring nature of God. Jesus proclaims:

> You have heard that it was said, "You shall love your neighbor and hate your enemy." But I say to you, love your enemies, bless those who curse you, do good to those who hate you, and pray for those who spitefully use you and persecute you, that you may be sons of your Father in heaven; for He makes His sun rise on the evil and on the good, and sends rain on the just and on the unjust. For if you love those who love you, what reward have you? Do not even the tax collectors do the same? And if you greet your brethren only, what do you do more than others? Do not even the tax collectors do so? Therefore you shall be perfect, just as your Father in heaven is perfect. (Matthew 5:43-48)

In a few short sentences, Jesus challenges us to love as He loves. Love those who make it difficult to love them. Love those who will never love us in return. Jesus calls us to love in the most challenging situations. He encourages us to

- Love those who hate us.
- Love those who curse us.
- Love those who persecute us.
- Love those who use us for their benefit.
- Love those who tease and mock us.
- Love those who humiliate us.
- Love those who wrong us.
- Love those who harm us.
- Love those who take advantage of us.

What an incredible challenge. He who loves in this way accrues no benefit. Consequently, such love makes the world take notice. God's love behaves differently than the worlds. Loving those who treat us horribly softens the hearts of our enemies. It makes them more receptive to the message of Jesus and piques their interest in learning more about the God we serve. If God's people express such selfless love, they wonder, how much more love must their God have? And so our tormentors often become our brothers when we show them love. Moreover, it captures the attention of the observing public. The world sees people showing love in the most trying circumstances and yearns for such love themselves. This creates opportunities to share our faith with a world desperate for genuine love.

Keep in mind this command does not represent a theoretical exercise. Jesus does not expect His followers to simply acknowledge such love intellectually. Moreover, He did not establish an impossible paradigm for His disciples to follow but refused to apply in His own life. As with every hard lesson He gave, Jesus exemplified it in His own life. He demonstrated love to each person with whom He came in contact, regardless of how they treated Him. The most dramatic example of this came on the day of His crucifixion. On that day, Jesus faced contempt, hatred, mocking, scourging, ridicule, violence, and, ultimately, death. Yet in each instance Jesus responded with love, compassion, and forgiveness. His example aligned with His message from years earlier and provided His adherents an unmistakable pattern to follow. Peter informs us, "Christ also suffered for us, leaving us an example, that you should follow His steps . . . who, when He was reviled did not revile in return; when He suffered, He did not threaten, but committed Himself to Him who judges righteously" (1 Peter 2:21, 23).

Paul echoes this challenge in advising us to "bless those who persecute you; bless and do not curse" (Romans 12:14). He later requires that we "repay no one evil for evil" (Romans 12:17). Paul reinforces Jesus' command to love our enemies and compels every believer to practice that love. When we love as Jesus did, we become more like Him and our relationship with Him deepens. As Jesus conducted His life as an example to His teachings, Paul did the same. On loving enemies, Paul and the apostles provided a living example: "Being reviled, we bless; being persecuted, we endure it; being defamed, we entreat" (1 Corinthians 4:12-13).

Peter builds on this foundation and informs us why we should respond in love to those who hate us, "not returning evil for evil or reviling for reviling, but on the contrary blessing, knowing that you were called to this, that you may inherit a blessing" (1 Peter 3:9). We behave with love because Jesus called us to such conduct. Our salvation exists because Jesus responded in love to those who hated Him, and He calls us to respond the same way. In doing so, Peter tells us we inherit a blessing in heaven.

As disciples of Jesus, we must love everyone including strangers and enemies. Our love extends to those who hurt us, hate us, despise us, and disrespect us. Jesus requires we love them substantively, sacrificially, and selflessly. Such love honors and glorifies God, attracts the world's attention (possibly providing an opportunity to witness), and differentiates disciples of Jesus from the world. It comforts, heals, and encourages a world stained by sin, hate, and hopelessness, and awakens the hardest heart to the genuine love of Jesus.

================================ QUESTIONS: ================================

1. Why does Jesus call us to love our enemies and those who hate us?

2. How does Jesus expect us to demonstrate love to strangers? How about to those who humiliate and persecute us?

3. These are extremely difficult commands. How do we substantively obey Jesus' directive to love strangers and enemies?

Jesus, knowing that the Father had given all things into His hands, and that He had come from God and was going to God, rose from supper and laid aside His garments, took a towel and girded Himself. After that, He poured water into a basin and began to wash the disciples' feet, and to wipe them with the towel with which He was girded. Then He came to Simon Peter. And Peter said to Him, "Lord, are You washing my feet?" Jesus answered and said to him, "What I am doing you do not understand now, but you will know after this." Peter said to Him, "You shall never wash my feet!" Jesus answered him, "If I do not wash you, you have no part with Me." Simon Peter said to Him, "Lord, not my feet only, but also my hands and my head!" Jesus said to him, "He who is bathed needs only to wash his feet, but is completely clean; and you are clean, but not all of you." For He knew who would betray Him; therefore He said, "You are not all clean." So when He had washed their feet, taken His garments, and sat down again, He said to them, "Do you know what I have done to you? You call Me Teacher and Lord, and you say well, for so I am. If I then, your Lord and Teacher, have washed your feet, you also ought to wash one another's feet. For I have given you an example, that you should do as I have done to you. Most assuredly, I say to you, a servant is not greater than his master; nor is he who is sent greater than he who sent him. If you know these things, blessed are you if you do them."

—John 13:3-17

CHAPTER 20

Serve

L ast chapter, we examined one of the most difficult challenges Jesus gave His disciples to follow. Loving strangers and enemies really tests the sincerity of our faith because it requires we live the Christian attributes of sacrifice, selflessness, and mercy. Such conduct demands real commitment to Jesus as Lord, for we cannot behave in such a manner on our strength alone.

Similarly, many of us have difficulty behaving with genuine humility and a servant's heart toward others. As before, Jesus provides an example we can mirror in living these attributes. He demonstrated both the night before His betrayal when He humbled Himself to wash the feet of His disciples, including the one who would betray Him.

No one aspires to wash feet for a living. There is nothing honorable about washing feet. In fact, the activity has numerous drawbacks. First, feet are filthy. The disciples walked everywhere in sandals. After a full day of walking you can imagine the amount of grime and filth on each of the apostles' feet. Second, feet stink. Without the benefit of socks and a good pair of walking shoes, I suspect the odor put off by each of the apostles' feet was quite strong. Third, washing feet puts the washer in a position of servitude. It requires considerable humility to stoop at another's feet to cleanse them. You cannot lord it over someone when washing his feet (see 1 Peter 5:1-3 where Peter exhorts elders to behave as shepherds and not as "lords over those entrusted to you, but [be] examples to the flock" (vs. 3)). Only the lowest servant would have to wash a master's feet. That was the entry level job of servitude, so to speak.

On the other hand (or foot), the receipt of a good foot washing after a long day walking undoubtedly refreshed each apostle. The feet of each disciple were likely tired and worn. Having them washed with cool water and then wiped and wrapped in a dry towel probably provided considerable comfort. Of course, Jesus' feet were also tired, dirty, and worn, yet He put the needs of His followers first. He modeled the behavior we must adopt as His disciples, to serve others and put their needs ahead of our own.

Perhaps the most powerful lesson in this story is Jesus' demonstration of humility. What a powerful image: our Creator coming as a man and washing the feet of His disciples. He exemplified how we need to operate with extreme humility, not a false or forced humility. The difference is the setting and the recognition. Do we look to serve in a public setting where others will credit us for having a servant's heart? Do we seek to show humility when others are watching? Such conduct contradicts the example Jesus provided. Jesus calls us to take on humbling tasks for which we receive no credit from others. Identify those needs in the church and community no one does because they are beneath everyone, and go do those first.

Paul challenges us to "let this mind be in you which was also in Christ Jesus, who . . . made Himself of no reputation, taking the form of a servant, and coming in the likeness of men. And being found in appearance as a man, He humbled Himself and became obedient to the point of death, even the death of the cross" (Philippians 2:5, 7-8). Jesus accomplished the will of the Father because He first counted Himself as having no reputation. Absent a reputation to maintain, Jesus need not concern Himself with the opinion of Pharisees, synagogue leaders, and society. He ignored the demands and compromises a reputation requires; He did not allow a reputation to enslave Him.

As a result, Jesus had the freedom to act with humility. He need not impress others by behaving like a big shot. He need not call attention to Himself to demonstrate His position or power. Unconcerned with His status, Jesus could focus entirely on the will of the Father. Armed with humility, Jesus prioritized service not power. The gospels provide example after example of Jesus serving others. He never sought someone to serve Him. Not once.

Paul encourages us to adopt that mindset: a singular focus on serving others, with humility. That burden to humbly serve others only occurs when we put to death our reputation and count it as loss. Paul informs us that serving others represents a product of our salvation. "For you, brethren, have been called to liberty; only do not use liberty as an opportunity for the flesh, but through love serve one another" (Galatians 5:13). Notice that through Christ we have liberty and through that liberty we have a choice; we can serve ourselves or we can serve others. Paul makes clear that we need to use the freedom in Christ to serve others as He did.

If we choose to put our own interests, lusts, and reputation first, what does that say about the validity of our faith? What does such behavior indicate about our relationship with Jesus? If we refuse to mirror His example, how can we honestly claim Him as Lord? If we do not serve others, we are not really serving Him. Service should be predicated on love—for the Lord and for others. Remember that in serving strangers sometimes we "unwittingly entertain angels" (Hebrews 13:2).

================ QUESTIONS: ================

1. Identify one or two actions you can take this week to serve someone or a group. What actions can you take to serve strangers in your community or those in another part of the world?

2. Why do you think Jesus places such an emphasis on serving others?

3. Can you think of recent examples when you have not acted with humility? Consider how you can adopt the humility that Jesus exemplified in His life.

Therefore the kingdom of heaven is like a certain king who wanted to settle accounts with his servants. And when he had begun to settle accounts, one was brought to him who owed him ten thousand talents. But as he was not able to pay, his master commanded that he be sold, with his wife and children and all that he had, and that payment be made. The servant therefore fell down before him, saying, "Master, have patience with me, and I will pay you all." Then the master of that servant was moved with compassion, released him, and forgave him the debt. But that servant went out and found one of his fellow servants who owed him a hundred denarii; and he laid hands on him and took him by the throat, saying, "Pay me what you owe!" So his fellow servant fell down at his feet and begged him, saying, "Have patience with me, and I will pay you all." And he would not, but went and threw him into prison till he should pay the debt. So when his fellow servants saw what had been done, they were very grieved, and came and told their master all that had been done. Then his master, after he had called him, said to him, "You wicked servant! I forgave you all that debt because you begged me. Should you not also have had compassion on your fellow servant, just as I had pity on you?" And his master was angry, and delivered him to the torturers until he should pay all that was due to him. So My heavenly Father also will do to you if each of you, from his heart, does not forgive his brother his trespasses.

—Matthew 18:23-35

CHAPTER 21

Forgive

Forgiveness is awesome, don't you think? Receiving someone's forgiveness for a wrong I commit is a really special experience. It restores the spirit. When forgiveness comes from Almighty God, it is even more amazing. That the God of the universe offers forgiveness for my wickedness is incomprehensible. I sometimes struggle to understand why He forgives, especially when I commit the same types of offenses over and over. Of course, forgiveness represents His nature.

Forgiveness, though, is not just a gift we receive; it is also a gift we must give. God calls us to extend forgiveness to everyone who has ever wronged us, irrespective of whether they recognize their wrong or ask for forgiveness. Of course, forgiveness is a lot easier to receive than it is to give. What makes it so easy to accept forgiveness and yet so difficult to offer it to others?

I think perspective accounts for much of the difference. When I fully understand the depths of my wickedness, the sin my heart harbors, the pride I possess, the selfishness I pursue, and the iniquity that consumes me, I appreciate more fully the breadth of Jesus' forgiveness. In contrast, when I perceive myself a decent guy, no worse than others, and who behaves pretty well, I incorrectly assume I need only modest forgiveness from God. I fail to comprehend the importance of Jesus' sacrifice. If I believe my life barely requires God's forgiveness, I will never understand the primary role grace plays in my salvation. Consequently, I will hesitate to extend grace to others.

Moreover, when I fail to understand the magnitude of Jesus' sacrifice to secure my forgiveness, I minimize His work on the cross. But when I grasp what His sacrifice cost, the pain, torture, and abuse He suffered on my behalf, I am more apt to extend mercy and forgiveness to others. Recognizing that He died the death I deserved, even though He had no blemish of sin, provides proper perspective so I can extend to others the mercy and forgiveness I have from Him. I must remember that if I withhold mercy and forgiveness from others, He will withhold His mercy and forgiveness from me.

Matthew captures the power of this principle in recounting Jesus' parable of the unforgiving servant, which He gave in response to Peter's question about the frequency we should forgive someone. As the master forgave his servant a debt he could not repay, so God forgives each believer a lifetime of sins for which no one can earn redemption. Salvation occurs because God bestows compassion and extends His mercy. We have no role in securing eternal life. What a relief. Spending eternity with the Lord is possible because He is gracious and merciful. His forgiveness restores us.

Like the servant, too often we fail to extend that mercy to others. We withhold forgiveness because someone wronged us and we want him to suffer the consequences. That was the perspective the forgiven servant adopted against his fellow servant. He tendered neither mercy nor forgiveness. He failed to comprehend that his master forgave a far greater debt than what his fellow servant owed. His selfishness and pride blinded him. He took for granted the mercy and forgiveness of his master but refused to apply that lesson to others. Because he failed to offer his fellow servant the grace he had received, the master revoked his forgiveness and mercy.

We often do the same thing. We want the mercy and grace Jesus offers but do not want to share those attributes with those who hurt us. However, remain mindful that the fate of the wicked servant awaits if we hold another captive for the wrong he commits against us and decline to forgive him. Listen to Jesus' words again. "So My heavenly Father also will do to you if each of you, from his heart, does not forgive his brother his trespasses" (Matthew 18:35).

God withholds forgiveness to those unwilling to forgive another, no matter the severity or frequency of the wrong. Like the servant in the parable, God does not allow us to accept His mercy and then refuse to extend that mercy to others. Notice that the forgiveness must come from the heart. It is not a flippant "I forgive you" while still harboring resentment, hate, and bitterness for the wrong. If sincere, forgiveness wipes the slate clean in our relationship with that person. We restore him even as Jesus restores us in our relationship with the Father. If we treat that person with ill will, remind him of his wrong, or allow the relationship to remain strained, then we have not fully forgiven. Forgiveness requires restoration.

Paul articulates this nexus between genuine forgiveness and how we treat the forgiven party. He reminds us to "let all bitterness, wrath, anger, clamor, and evil speaking be put away from you, with all malice. And be kind to one another, tenderhearted, forgiving one another, just as God in Christ also forgave you" (Ephesians 4:31-32). We forgive because Christ forgave us first. As our Lord, we model His example of forgiveness. And what does a relationship look like with someone you have forgiven? It is marked by kindness and compassion. You genuinely care about that person. You set aside all emotion that erupted when he sinned against you. No more anger. No more bitterness. No more plotting revenge. No more destroying his reputation and disparaging him around others. Forgiveness requires you set aside those sinful responses and replace them with love.

Paul reiterates this point with the church at Colossae. He counsels them to "[forgive] one another, if anyone has a complaint against another; even as Christ forgave you, so you also must do" (Colossians 3:13). Forgiveness is not optional. Anyone who experienced God's mercy does not get to withhold it from others. Paul exclaims we "must" forgive anyone who has wronged us in any manner. God requires it. There are several reasons we must forgive. It restores the one who committed the wrong. It prevents bitterness, anger, and revenge from destroying us or driving us to wicked behavior. It contrasts dramatically with how the world responds in similar situations and so provides society insight into God's forgiveness. It is a testimony of the mercy God extends to every sinner. It demonstrates the power He furnishes His people, that they are able to forgive others.

In Acts, Stephen the martyr demonstrated genuine forgiveness. He suffered a brutal death of stoning at the hands of those with whom he sought to share the good news of Jesus. But his bold testimony and witness infuriated them and they responded to him with violence. As they attacked him and beat him with stones, he looked toward heaven and petitioned the Father on their behalf, "Lord, do not charge them with this sin" (Acts 7:60). In the midst of his pain, suffering, and death, Stephen's concern was for his killers, that God would extend them mercy.

Offering forgiveness can be difficult, especially when the wrong is severe and unspeakable. Stephen forgave because his concern for the souls of his tormenters outweighed his concern for his own well-being. He desired to see his abusers become his brothers in the Lord so he forgave them. In the process, he gave them a glimpse of the Father's forgiveness and mercy. Adopting that perspective makes it easier to forgive anyone who wrongs us.

═══════════════════ QUESTIONS: ═══════════════════

1. What makes forgiveness so difficult to extend others? How does genuine forgiveness look?

2. Is there anyone you need to forgive? What prevents you from forgiving him or her today?

3. Why does God call us to forgive others and extend them grace?

And Jesus came and spoke to them, saying, 'All authority has been given to Me in heaven and on earth. Go therefore and make disciples of all the nations, baptizing them in the name of the Father and of the Son and of the Holy Spirit, teaching them to observe all things that I have commanded you; and lo, I am with you always, even to the end of the age.' Amen.

—Matthew 28:18-20

CHAPTER 22

Testify

Sharing our faith in Jesus can be difficult for many of us. We do not want friends to think we are overly religious. We want to avoid a topic many of our colleagues and neighbors have little interest in or hold with contempt. We resist proclaiming our faith to a culture increasingly hostile to the name of Jesus and to those who call Him Lord.

But God calls us to discuss our faith with others and challenges us to share how He is at work in our lives. He requires we inform others of the love, mercy, and forgiveness He offers a damaged world. Jesus gave the disciples the Great Commission when they met with Him following His resurrection. It applies to every believer who confesses Him as Lord. Fulfilling His command to reach all people with His message of love involves four requirements:

1. Go.
2. Make disciples.
3. Baptize.
4. Teach.

We pursue each of these on the strength and authority of Jesus Christ. And pursue them we must. They are not optional to the Christian faith. No genuine believer ignores them. Jesus calls us to fulfill them because He desires the entire world hear His good news and have the opportunity to respond. As His saints, we are the messengers He uses to bring a message of hope and salvation to a broken world. How do we obey His command?

We go! Whether across the room to a family member, across the street to a neighbor, across town to a stranger, or across the world to someone unlike us, we must go. While only a few of us leave the United States to fulfill the command, we all must go somewhere and each of us must go to someone. Refusing to go reveals a spirit of rebellion. It exposes the selfishness that continues to reside in the heart. If you will not go to others and share your faith, you are living in disobedience.

It is no excuse to explain your ineloquence. God does not require eloquence. He only requires obedience. Claiming your personality precludes sharing your faith is an invalid reason. You are not going on your own strength but on His. Asserting that others will not listen or that you know they have no interest is an unacceptable justification for refusing to go. Jesus does not require that those to whom you go respond favorably or even express interest. He commands you go regardless of their response.

We make disciples. As we share Jesus' love and good news with others, some will embrace His message. We disciple them by building a spiritual foundation grounded in a robust relationship with the Lord. We help them understand what the call of Christ represents and explain how to live as a disciple of Jesus. We equip them with an understanding of God's word and cultivate in them a passion for studying it. We assist them in comprehending the character and person of Jesus, and challenge them to become more like Him.

We baptize. Baptism provides each believer the platform for making a public profession of faith and represents an opportunity to tell his family, friends, and associates that he is a new person. No longer will he pursue the worldly path he previously followed. While you might not conduct the baptism, you need to communicate to the believer the criticality of announcing his faith to the world.

We teach. We instruct new believers to follow Jesus and His commands. Jesus taught many lessons to the crowds and his followers, and we must teach all of them as well. We cannot selectively teach only those insights with which we agree. We must avoid excluding those teachings that the culture deems offensive. We cannot teach only those lessons that are easy to implement. We must teach everything Jesus taught since each lesson represents eternal truth.

We do this in obedience. We obey because a loving God calls us to share His love with a hateful world. In obeying, we demonstrate boldness. Boldness does not mean adopting an angry posture or operating with excess aggressiveness. Rather, we evidence boldness when we share with gentleness, kindness, and love. Because the world is at war with Jesus and the Christian faith, simply fulfilling the commands of Jesus to go, disciple, baptize, and teach shows boldness.

Some will say they are too afraid to share the good news. But Scripture tells us "there is no fear in love" because "perfect love casts out fear" (1 John 4:18). God's love compels us to share His love, mercy, and truth with others. We share His desire to see all people come to salvation. His love removes the fear of rejection, of ridicule, of wrath, and of hatred the world may heap on us in response to sharing Jesus with them. We may still suffer those consequences, but we do not fear them because His love for us and for others compels us to share. His love removes our fear.

Some suggest they are too timid to share the good news. Scripture refutes this rationale as well, telling us, "God has not given us a spirit of fear and timidity, but of power, love, and self-discipline" (2 Timothy 1:7, New Living Translation). We operate with power, love, and self-discipline as followers of God, not with fear or timidity. The Holy Spirit equips us with this power. When we submit to Jesus as Lord, He sends the Holy Spirit who empowers us to do the will of God. He gives us the attributes necessary to fulfill the work to which He has called us.

To fulfill the Great Commission, we need boldness. He gives us that, no matter our personality, disposition, or "how we are wired." We read in Acts how the early church evidenced this boldness. "After this prayer, the meeting place shook, and they were all filled with the Holy Spirit. Then they preached the word of God with boldness" (Acts 4:31, NLT). The Holy Spirit's presence permitted them to preach with boldness. He does the same for each believer. If you remain convinced that you lack the boldness and power to share Jesus with your friends, neighbors, and strangers, ask the Lord to grant you the attributes necessary. As with the early church, He will provide you power and boldness through the Holy Spirit (Acts 4:29).

Of course, sharing truth does not always result in the audience receiving the message favorably. Sometimes those to whom we preach will respond with anger, persecution and resistance. Paul often confronted such responses but remained steadfast in sharing. He told the Thessalonica church, "For you yourselves know, brethren, that our coming to you was not in vain. But even after we had suffered before and were spitefully treated at Philippi, as you know, we were bold in our God to speak to you the gospel of God in much conflict" (1 Thessalonians 2:1-2). Paul models the resilience we should demonstrate. We must persevere and continue to share truth. Even in the face of hateful treatment we must remain steadfast in discussing the good news with others.

While society may ridicule us, we have confidence that God's word validates the truth of Jesus as Savior. Jesus affirmed, "I am the way, the truth, and the life. No one comes to Father except through Me" (John 14:6). Peter informed the high priest, rulers, and elders that salvation comes through Jesus alone, saying, "Nor is there salvation in any other, for there is no other name under heaven given among men by which we must be saved" (Acts 4:12). These verses leave no room for suggesting another path to heaven exists. All other routes place the burden on man to earn in some manner his salvation. But the Bible teaches salvation by grace alone and that no amount of works will suffice since "all our righteous acts are as filthy rags" (Isaiah 64:6, NIV). Armed with the biblical support for the truth of Jesus as Savior, we can share with assurance the hope and sacrifice of Christ.

God calls us to share this truth with as many people as possible. We should seek to share with someone each day; pray the Lord will provide the opportunity. When opportunities arise, we should discuss the path of salvation, God's mercy, and how Jesus' sacrifice covers our sins, allowing us to fellowship directly with God. Paul challenges us to, "Preach the word! Be ready in season and out of season. Convince, rebuke, exhort, with all longsuffering and teaching" (2 Timothy 4:2). Are you prepared to share the good news of Jesus with anyone who asks?

1. Do you explore opportunities to share Jesus and His love with others regularly? If not, why?

2. God calls us to make disciples as part of the Great Commission. Are you discipling anyone? What does it mean to disciple someone?

3. Jesus' love removes our fear and timidity. How does that biblical truth encourage you to adopt a bolder posture in sharing Jesus with others? What does it mean to share your faith boldly?

give them warning from Me: When I say to the wicked, 'You shall surely die,' and you give him no warning, nor speak to warn the wicked from his wicked way, to save his life, that same wicked man shall die in his iniquity; but his blood I will require at your hand. Yet, if you warn the wicked, and he does not turn from his wickedness, nor from his wicked way, he shall die in his iniquity; but you have delivered your soul. Again, when a righteous man turns from his righteousness and commits iniquity, and I lay a stumbling block before him, he shall die; because you did not give him warning, he shall die in his sin, and his righteousness which he has done shall not be remembered; but his blood I will require at your hand. Nevertheless if you warn the righteous man that the righteous should not sin, and he does not sin, he shall surely live because he took warning; also you will have delivered your soul.

—Ezekiel 3:17-21

CHAPTER 23

Correct

Amerian culture increasingly emphasizes tolerance. It advocates treating all philosophies as equally legitimate. No perspective reigns supreme according to this worldview. Society views with contempt any belief that holds itself superior to other beliefs. Culture holds particular animosity against any religion that presumes to possess truth at the exclusion of other faiths. Since Scripture asserts Jesus Christ as the only path to salvation, society perceives Christianity as especially dangerous and despicable. That God's Word teaches the existence of sin and evil only amplifies its villainy in the eyes of the world, which resists recognizing any behavior as sinful.

As social opposition against biblical Christianity has increased, especially in the halls of academia and among the intelligentsia, the American church has begun to shift its treatment of sin, ungodliness, and worldliness. Rather than preach against sinful behavior and challenging believers to hold each other accountable in conduct, the church increasingly emphasizes tolerance. Adopting a cultural posture, many American churches now label as judgmental any effort by believers to hold one another to God's standard of godliness and holiness. Such churches align with the cultural view that you should "not judge, that you be not judged."

While most people have no idea the biblical source for this admonition (it is found in Matthew 7:1), nor the context in which Jesus used it, they have supreme confidence that it precludes any Christian from telling a fellow believer the inappropriateness of his behavior. No matter how wicked or how harmful the behavior, the modern ideal of tolerance requires acceptance. Referring to any behavior as sin, or challenging another person to repent from ungodly behavior, is now viewed as the only sin we must avoid. Christians who attempt to correct or admonish their spiritual brothers and sisters for any ongoing sin demonstrate a judgmental spirit and an air of superiority. So claims the culture and an increasing number of churches.

With such resistance emanating from a greater segment of the church and the broader culture, obeying God in such situations often proves difficult. As society demonizes anyone who believes in eternal truth, who upholds a biblical standard for right and wrong, and who labels ungodly behavior as sin, speaking scriptural truth becomes a challenge. Those who do must fight considerable headwinds from society and often from the church.

But Scripture teaches our need to correct an erring brother. Pointing out the biblical proscription for sinful behavior practiced by a believer and challenging him to repent from such conduct aligns with what Jesus taught. Numerous verses address God's mandate that we not ignore any believer living in sin or preaching untruths. Let's explore several passages that tackle this topic.

With respect to those who have wandered from the truth, James encourages us to restore them from their sin. "Brethren, if anyone among you wanders from the truth, and someone turns him back, let him know that he who turns a sinner from the error of his way will save a soul from death and cover a multitude of sins" (James 5:19-20). Helping a fellow believer get back on track spiritually results in restoration. Whenever we confront a believer over his practice of sinful behavior and encourage him to repent, we do him a considerable favor. The sinning brother who repents and ceases his lifestyle of sin benefits enormously.

Of course, we must adopt the proper posture in approaching a believer living in sin. Paul advises us, "Brethren, if a man is overtaken in any trespass, you who are spiritual restore such a one in a spirit of gentleness, considering yourself lest you also be tempted" (Galatians 6:1). Paul does not equivocate on the issue of whether to correct the brother who has fallen into a lifestyle of sin. We must. It represents our spiritual duty. His counsel addresses how we go about restoring that sinning brother. He encourages us to put on a spirit of gentleness. Adopting a brash tone or a coarse posture likely will yield unproductive results. It may result in the sinning brother taking a much more defensive stance; consequently, he may have little receptivity to your intervention.

Similarly, displaying an arrogant disposition offers little likelihood for success when correcting another. No one wants to receive correction from someone who views himself better than you. So Paul encourages us to correct with humility. Make sure your body language and tone reflect genuine care for the person. Moreover, he reminds us to consider our own weaknesses. Realize we too have our own tendencies to sin. When we correct a sinning believer with an arrogant attitude, spiritual pride builds up in us. That pride is exceptionally dangerous, for it leads to the fall (see Proverbs 16:18) and represents an abomination before God (see Proverbs 6:16-17). Speaking with arrogance heightens the likelihood you succumb to sin as well. Perhaps not the same type of sin, but pride leads to falling more easily to sin.

Of course, not everyone responds to a gentle rebuke. Some individuals require a more direct and assertive tone and conversation. Jude challenges us to distinguish between those who respond to a gentle correction and those who need a more candid and forceful censure. He tells us, "And on some have compassion, making a distinction; but others save with fear, pulling them out of the fire, hating even the garment defiled by the flesh" (Jude 1:22-23). Regarding chastisement, most of us prefer to receive a gentle rebuke from someone we know cares about us. Jude tells us to display a compassionate disposition in correcting such people. Make sure they understand the gravity and error of their sin, but do so with gentleness. In contrast, some will move so quickly down the path of destruction that only an adamant and vigorous rebuke will wake them. They are on the cusp of judgment and require immediate awareness of their sin. Make a distinction for such sinning brothers, under the leadership of the Holy Spirit, and employ the more assertive approach.

Regarding the topic of correcting a wayward believer, keep in mind the Bible refers to fellow believers who are practicing sin. We are not told to observe every Christian around us and correct each of them every time one commits a single sin. Scripture commands us to address those fellow disciples of Jesus who have fallen into a lifestyle of sin; those who have embraced sinful behavior and incorporated it into their regular life. These verses do not give us a license to tell every believer their shortcomings. It requires we confront a brother committing a pattern of sin. We must allow the Holy Spirit to guide our approach, words, and tone so we optimize the likelihood our brother repents.

This requirement does not rest with Christian leaders alone. Paul tells us that every servant of the Lord must "in humility correct those who are in opposition, if God perhaps will grant them repentance, so that they may know the truth, and that they may come to their senses and escape the snare of the devil, having been taken captive by him to do his will" (2 Timothy 2:25-26). Each believer has a duty to correct those opposing the truth in conduct and in speech. Not everyone we confront will repent; that result rests entirely with the Lord. But He requires we correct them and He holds us accountable for whether we do. He outlines this expectation in His message to Ezekiel at the top of the chapter

God expects us to warn the wicked of his impending judgment unless he repents. God wants us to return the lost back to Him. But we disobey when we refuse to speak truth and correct others. As a result, the wicked perish. They remain in their sin and never develop a personal relationship with God. We have the opportunity to prevent someone from going to hell for eternity, but too often we ignore it and allow him to suffer eternal damnation. It is sad that so many of us are more concerned with our worldly reputations and getting along with people than we are with eternal souls. We place our social status of greater importance than the eternal destination of many friends, colleagues, and strangers who are lost.

But the consequence of failing to share the truth with others does not apply to the sinner alone. It falls on each of us. God tells us He will require the blood of the wicked at our hands. For each lost person with whom we come into contact and do not share the gospel, God holds us accountable. He also requires we correct the righteous who fall into sin; those brothers and sisters in Christ who succumb to temptation and follow a pattern of sin risk God's judgment. If we fail to warn them, God remembers their righteous deeds no more, but He holds us accountable for their blood as well.

Few people want to correct a brother living in sin. It is difficult to initiate a conversation in which you explain that the lifestyle of a fellow believer is sinful. It is much easier to go along to get along. We do not point out the pattern of sin in the lives of others, and they extend us the same courtesy. While this approach finds strong support in our culture, it has no basis in Scripture. God calls us to rebuke the sinning brother with a spirit of gentleness that he might repent and have a restored relationship with the Lord. Despite the difficulty, we must do this as our Christian duty.

=== QUESTIONS: ===

1. Jesus commands us not to judge yet Scripture also tells us to correct a believer who practices sin. How do we reconcile these two positions?

2. Why is it so important to correct with meekness a believer who falls away from the faith?

3. Do you find it difficult to correct a believer living a lifestyle of sin? What can you do to ensure you obey God in this area?

You ask and do not receive because you ask amiss that you may spend it on your own pleasures.

—James 4:3

CHAPTER 24

Pray

One lens into the condition of the heart is our prayer life. Prayer reflects our priorities, passions, and what we treasure. We focus prayer on those people who matter most to us, those situations that most concern us, and for those things which we care about the most. If you want to know whether you have a selfish faith, consider the content of your prayers. For a candid assessment of the sincerity of your faith, reflect on the frequency and substance of your prayer. The emphasis of your prayers provides an unvarnished glance into the maturity and authenticity of your faith.

- Prayers emphasizing "you" indicate a selfish faith.
- Prayers focusing on the cares of this world suggest a temporal faith.
- Prayers petitioning God for His material blessing imply a greedy faith.
- Prayers addressing family, friends, and loved ones reflect a parochial faith.

Many of us focus our prayers primarily on three subjects: ourselves, family, and friends. Sadly, God often comes in fourth, with praise and worship an afterthought. Meanwhile, strangers, the persecuted church, and the unsaved often are not even on the prayer radar for many believers. Moreover, we spend too little of our private prayer praising the Lord for who He is, direct few prayers on supporting the work the Holy Spirit is accomplishing around the world in bringing millions into a relationship with God, and invest too little prayer time on revival in this country.

Before we explore what our prayer focus indicates about our faith, take a few minutes to honestly assess your prayer life. Consider the following questions and note your candid answer next to each. You need not share your responses with others, but you should record your answers to better grasp the current state of your heart and recognize the need for future growth in this area.

1. How much time a week do you spend in prayer (on average, since every week is different)?

2. What percentage focuses on you and your needs?

3. What percentage lifts up friends and family?

4. What percentage do you direct toward strangers, such as the unsaved, the persecuted church, missionaries, and the needy?

5. What percentage glorifies the Lord and worships God?

6. With respect to prayers for yourself, your family, and your friends, what percentage centers around spiritual growth and becoming like Christ, and what percent centers on temporal needs (health, job, school, intervention in difficult situations, material blessings)?

Our prayers should first and foremost focus on God and Jesus. We should offer prayers of thanksgiving for His many blessings, prayers of praise for His character and righteousness, and prayers of submission to His Lordship. We ought to worship Him as well, expressing our devotion, recognizing Him as Creator, and affirming Him as the source of all good things.

We should then focus on others, particularly those with spiritual needs. We should pray for those who have never heard the gospel, perhaps even adopting a specific people group or country for whom we can pray regularly. We should pray for our fellow believers who suffer persecution around the world, often subject to physical beatings, jail time, loss of employment, and even death. Pray that God would encourage them and remind them of His promise to reward them for their faithfulness. We should pray for those without access to Bibles, infrequent access to sound biblical teaching, and those denied the freedom to worship or fellowship. Pray that the Lord would provide the tools and training so believers everywhere can grow closer to Him and strengthen their faith; ask God to show how you can participate in this. We should pray for those with physical needs such as malnutrition, loneliness, unsafe drinking water, and easily prevented illnesses, especially fellow believers who lack basic necessities. Seek the Lord's leadership on how you can help meet these needs.

We should pray for friends and families, especially their spiritual needs such as spiritual maturity, a bolder faith, and, if unsaved, their salvation. Talk with your friends and family members and ask what spiritual needs they have: more holiness, boldness, stronger prayer life, power over a specific sin, a passion for God's word, etc. Then pray with regularity for God to provide these.

After you have praised and worshipped God, prayed for the unsaved, the needs of other believers, the less fortunate, and your loved ones, then focus your remaining prayers on yourself. They should represent a small portion of your prayer. Moreover, those prayers should focus on your spiritual growth first. Ask God to fill your heart with a greater love for Him each day. Ask Him to grant you genuine humility. Seek His godliness in your life. Ask that He equip you with a generous heart so you direct more of your resources to fulfilling His will. If you pattern your prayer life in such a manner, you will notice an increased focus on things of eternal value that align with God's heart.

For too long we have believed we can pray for ourselves, our plans, and our agenda and that God will answer those according to our wishes. We have embraced the perspective that God hears and answers our prayers no matter how selfish and worldly. False teaching has deceived us into the view that God yearns to meet not only our needs but also our worldly desires. Scripture offers a much more radical view of prayer. Let's examine God's word to discern how we ought to pray and understand when God answers our prayer.

John tells us in his first epistle, "Now this is the confidence that we have in Him, that if we ask anything according to His will He hears us" (1 John 5:14). John emphasizes the point that Jesus hears our prayers. We can believe this with confidence. The only caveat John provides is that our petitions align with His will; self-seeking prayers are excluded. So what is God's will? According to Scripture, it is our sanctification (see 1 Thessalonians 4:3), our spiritual growth, a compassionate heart, a burden for the lost, boldness in our faith; and wisdom to preach

God's love. Only when we pray according to His will does He hear our prayers.

Jesus said, "Whatever you ask in My name, that I will do that the Father may be glorified in the Son. If you ask anything in My name, I will do it" (John 14:13-14). Many of us read this verse and believe it gives us a license to make any request of the Lord and He will spring into action. But Jesus indicates He answers our requests to glorify the Father. So how is the Father glorified? "By this My Father is glorified, that you bear much fruit" (John 15:8). Our faithfulness bears fruit for the Lord and glorifies the Father. When our petitions seek opportunities to bear more fruit, He fulfills our requests. When we ask for spiritual maturity, victory over sin, growth in spiritual attributes, and becoming more like Christ, then the Father is glorified. Such prayer receives an audience and answer from God because it results in increased fruitfulness in our lives.

The psalmist declares that if you "delight yourself also in the Lord," "He shall give you the desires of your heart" (Psalm 37:4). God answers prayer and provides you the desires of your heart. However, He first requires you delight yourself in Him. That prerequisite makes all the difference. If you pursue the presence of God and His attributes, then you will desire those things He desires. You will not desire selfish things but that which brings glory to God and advances His will. One cannot delight himself in the Lord and simultaneously harbor sinful desires. He gives us our desires when our desires mirror His, and that occurs when we delight ourselves with His presence.

Similarly, John observes, "And whatever we ask we receive from Him, because we keep His commandments, and do those things that are pleasing in His sight" (1 John 3:22). Mirroring the observation of the psalmist, John affirms that God grants our requests. But once again a condition exists. John says we must keep the commandments of God and perform those actions that please Him. Of course, it is impossible to keep God's commands and please Him unless we have a heart after His own. Such a heart offers prayers that honor Him and are not self-serving. The prayers of those who obey and please God focus on others

211

and not ourselves. They focus on advancing His kingdom rather than our selfish agenda. They focus on the unsaved, the hurting, and on revival.

What desires does one have if he delights himself in the Lord and keeps His commands? The psalmist tells us, "One thing I have desired of the Lord, that I will seek: That I may dwell in the house of the Lord all the days of my life to behold the beauty of the Lord and to inquire in His temple" (Psalm 27:4). That perspective reflects the heart of one who loves God. He delights in being in the presence of God and finds pleasure in having a relationship with the Lord. He does not seek pleasure from the things of this world or joy from temporal things. When our prayers reflect this yearning, God gives us the desires of our heart.

Jesus affirms this saying, "If you abide in Me, and My words abide in you, you will ask what you desire and it shall be done for you" (John 15:7). Again, the Lord gives us the desires of our heart but only if we abide in Him and His words abide in us. If Jesus truly abides in our heart, we will not pray selfish prayers. We will not seek His blessing on ourselves but on others. We will not seek more of this world but more of the Holy Spirit. Moreover, His words cannot abide in us if we do not read His word. It is preposterous to think God's words reside in us if we rarely read the Bible. Of course, as we consume the Word of God with greater passion and frequency our lives invariably change. Our thoughts, priorities, and desires become like His. As they do, He fulfills our petitions and requests.

We now understand when God hears and fulfills our prayer petitions. But what accounts for those prayers of ours that remain unanswered? James explains the probable cause of such prayers. "You ask and do not receive because you ask amiss that you may spend it on your own pleasures" (James 4:3). Does your prayer life encounter little success? Consider the truth of James's observation. When we pray selfish prayers, the Lord refuses to honor them. He declines to grant our requests when we seek our own pleasure.

James explains why so many of our prayers go unanswered. They reflect a greedy heart. Our requests spring from our lusts and represent the desires of our flesh. Most of us have prayed these types of prayers at some point in life. They are completely consumed with self and benefit no one else. Often such prayers seek temporal outcomes not spiritual ones. Such requests should not reflect our primary (or even secondary) focus in prayer. Even the most innocuous prayer is wicked if it is predicated on satisfying the will of the flesh. So we must get to the root of our prayers as they relate to ourselves. Whose will do we hope to fulfill? Who do we hope is glorified if the prayer is answered? How will we use the benefit that accrues if God answers our prayer?

Our prayer lives operate as an accurate mirror into our hearts and demonstrate what we treasure. From them we identify our true love. They describe clearly the condition of our faith. What do your prayers say about your faith? What do they reveal about your relationship with Jesus? What priorities, passions, and focus do your prayers represent?

1. Why does God place conditions on us before He answers our prayers?

2. What does your prayer life indicate about your heart? Does it demonstrate a desire to know Him and make Him known, or a love for the world?

3. How can you ensure God's words abide in you? What impact will that have on your life?

PART VI

Difficult because: We Suffer Persecution

One of the most difficult consequences of the Christian faith is persecution. Unlike many of the other ways our faith is difficult, persecution often includes suffering in some form or another. Persecution covers many acts that involve mental, emotional, and physical abuse. Remaining faithful and living boldly for Jesus often results in the believer suffering a loss as well—loss of freedom, loss of job, loss of social position. Our brothers and sisters in developing countries tend to experience persecution more frequently and severely than we do in the United States. In many Asian and Middle Eastern countries, in fact, harsh persecution is a certainty.

What role does persecution play in the believer's faith? Does God use persecution to accomplish His purposes, and if so what are those purposes? More pointedly, why does God allow His people to suffer through the pain and trials of persecution? Does the presence of persecution indicate anything about the faith of the believers who suffer it? Should we express concern that we experience very little persecution in the United States?

The next three chapters explore these questions. We examine Scripture to understand who suffers persecution and why it exists. We address why people and governments persecute believers, and how God facilitates His will through persecution. Lastly, we consider how Scripture advises us to respond to persecution. You will likely find the biblical approach difficult to digest, and even more difficult to implement—which is not surprising, since the path that leads to life is difficult.

Yes, and all who desire to live godly in Christ Jesus will suffer persecution.

—2 Timothy 3:12

CHAPTER 25

Who Suffers Persecution

Persecution of believers exists in some form or another in just about every country where the Christian faith exists. While it tends to occur with more severity in Asian and North African countries where the majority of citizens practice Islam, Hinduism, or Buddhism, it happens in only the mildest forms in the United States, perhaps verbal ridicule or expressed contempt, but rarely does an American believer suffer physical harm or jail for his faith.

In fact, most of us probably think we are immune to persecution because we live in the United States. We believe First Amendment protection of religious freedom precludes our suffering for the cause of Christ. Scripture, though, offers no exclusion to persecution. It states that anyone who follows Jesus as a disciple will suffer persecution. There are no exceptions. Every believer will face tribulation in some form or another due to his faith.

Paul tells Timothy, "Yes, and *all* who desire to live godly in Christ Jesus *will* suffer persecution" (2 Timothy 3:12, emphasis added). He understood that suffering for the cause of Christ was not optional. His message to Timothy leaves no doubt. Everyone who follows the pattern of godliness established by Jesus suffers persecution. No one is exempt. Paul does not view persecution as a possibility or even a likelihood. It is a certainty.

How can Paul assert that absolute claim? How can he know without doubt that all believers will face persecution? He knew the eternal enmity between the world and God would always drive persecution. This world hates godliness because it contrasts with the permissiveness and immorality the world embraces. That contrast magnifies the world's sinful behavior, and the world loathes the idea that sin exists. Moreover, holy lives point to a God who will hold all accountable for their conduct and the world abhors the concept of accountability. This ongoing tension between a wicked world and a holy God fuels the animosity society holds for the Church. The world views God's people with the same contempt it views the Lord Himself. That contempt drives the persecution the world heaps upon those who seek to honor God, live godly and glorify Jesus.

Persecution comes in different forms and varies by setting and parties involved. It includes mocking and belittling; spreading rumors and making false accusations; loss of employment or getting passed over for a promotion; rejection from friends and family; violence and bodily harm; destruction of property; getting jailed for beliefs; and even martyrdom. For American Christians, persecution almost never involves the last four on the list, although the time is rapidly approaching when it will.

So what does it mean if we do not suffer persecution for our faith? The verse above clearly stipulated that you suffer if you live godly in Jesus. Ask yourself then, are you living godly? Do you seek godliness in all situations—such as around your friends and at work? Do you take bold stands for Jesus? Do you speak up for righteousness and link it back to your faith? Do you speak God's truth when an opportunity arises?

Too often we display timidity in our faith. We prefer to leave things unsaid when a topic arises that invites drawing a distinction between the world's view and Jesus'. So we just keep our mouths shut. Better to avoid sharing our faith than risk getting teased for our views, or mocked as a religious extremist, or accused of being closed-minded.

But Jesus said we are a light unto the world that shines in the darkness (see Matthew 5:14-16). How can the light shine, He asks, if you cover it? We do exactly that when we choose to keep silent during a discussion that lends itself to sharing Jesus and biblical truth. Discussions about movies, television shows, current events, office drama, and politics often raise issues of sexual immorality, universalism (that all faiths lead to God), and boorish language. Does your life contrast with the lives of those in the world on these issues? Does your conduct, work ethic, speech, and servant-heart draw a contrast with your friends', colleagues', and neighbors'? Not a judgmental, better-than-thou posture, but a contrast that invites dialogue around Jesus and His Lordship in your life.

If you experience little to no persecution, then it probably indicates your life contrasts too little with the world. It may suggest that you take the easy path of compromise. Be bold in your faith and you will find yourself subject to increased persecution with increased intensity. Do not allow such treatment to surprise you. Jesus said, "And you *will* be hated by all for My name's sake" (Matthew 10:22a, emphasis added).

The persecution the world directs at us it first directed at Jesus. If we share in His glory, we must also share in His suffering. Peter stressed, "For to this you were called, because Christ also suffered for us, leaving us an example, that you should follow His steps" (1 Peter 2:21). We cannot decouple persecution from discipleship. Paul emphasized this in his epistle to the Philippians. "For to you it has been granted on behalf of Christ, not only to believe in Him, but also to suffer for His sake" (Philippians 1:29). Those who believe will suffer for the Lord. This is not a punishment but a gift. Paul says God grants us the opportunity to suffer for Christ as part of our faith. Similarly, Paul informs us, "You therefore must endure hardship as a good soldier of Jesus Christ" (2 Timothy 2:3). Suffering and persecution represent a normal outcome of living for Jesus, if indeed we follow and obey Him as a good soldier.

As followers of Jesus we must recognize that persecution will occur. Paul told the church at Derbe, "We must through many tribulations enter the kingdom of God" (Acts 14:22b). Americans are not exempt. Having an understanding of this truth and why God allows it will strengthen us to persevere when it happens.

1. Does it seem unreasonable that God would allow all who follow Him to suffer persecution?

2. Have you experienced persecution? In what ways?

3. Should the absence of persecution concern a believer? What does it indicate?

That the genuineness of your faith, being much more precious than gold that perishes, though it is tested by fire, may be found to praise, honor, and glory at the revelation of Jesus Christ.

—1 Peter 1:7

CHAPTER 26

Why Persecution Occurs

God uses persecution to test and refine our faith. As we suffer persecution, one of two things happens. Our faith grows, we become more mature in our relationship with the Lord, and we live more boldly for Him. Alternatively, we fall away, reject the Lord, and return to our life in the world.

Persecution often yields explosive church growth as believers mature in their faith very quickly. In addition, Christians who respond with love and kindness to severe forms of persecution provide a compelling example to the world. That often leads multitudes to Jesus who want the joy, peace, and grace they see in the lives of those who suffer persecution. So not only does persecution develop spiritual growth in the individual and community of believers, it also grows the church by attracting new believers.

In the alternative outcome, a faux believer leaves the faith due to persecution. He does not lose his salvation but demonstrates he never possessed genuine faith at all. The persecution simply revealed him for the imposter he was. He claimed the Christian faith but did not truly believe in his heart. Jesus identifies such people as those who "hear the word [and] immediately receive it with gladness; and they have no root in themselves, and so endure only for a time. Afterward, when tribulation or persecution arises for the word's sake, immediately they stumble" (Mark 4:16-17).

Persecution, then, helps purify the church and remove the tares (who are false believers). In fact, insufficient persecution correlates with an increase of tares in the church. They possess insincere faith that revolves around self rather than focuses on God. These carnal Christians corrupt the church, establish the commandments of men as doctrine, and begin the decay of the church body so it eventually loses its power (see Jude 1). They are identified throughout Scripture, and we will examine them more closely in chapter 30. Suffice it to say, we need a robust level of persecution to minimize the number of false believers "playing church."

In fact, the American church desperately needs persecution so the Lord can rid her of the considerable number of tares who have crept in for decades and corrupted the truth. Keep in mind that increased persecution results as the contrast grows more dramatic between culture and truth. The absence of significant persecution in the United States reveals too little contrast between the church and our culture. But as persecution increases, the boldness of believers will increase as well (see Ephesians 6:19-20), further sharpening the contrast with culture. That boldness will heighten interest from a world desperate for meaning and purpose. Persecution will also lead the American church to adopt a more biblical lifestyle that impacts our communities more powerfully, and equip us with a greater urgency in communicating the gospel.

Paul tells us to "glory in tribulation" since it "produces perseverance; and perseverance, character; and character, hope" (Romans 5:3-4). Persecution equips us to persevere when additional trials come our way. We learn to trust more fully in the Lord. By experience we discover that in the midst of difficulties and tribulation God provides for us and draws us to Him. In addition, our character matures and we more accurately reflect Jesus and His attributes. Finally, we acquire hope. Hope of things to come and hope for His promises. Especially evident in countries where violence and governmental persecution runs rampant, hope strengthens believers in difficult and painful circumstances; they rely heavily on the hope of Christ's return and the promise of heaven.

In America, our hope for "the things to come" does not manifest itself so clearly. An absence of substantive persecution dulls our ability to persevere and dilutes our hope for a future with Jesus. We do not develop those attributes as fully as fellow believers in Muslim and Buddhist countries. Our diminished development of those attributes represents another reason we need greater persecution in this country; so we sharpen our perseverance and our hope for things to come.

Building on this, Paul observes, "For our light affliction, which is but for a moment, is working for us a far more exceeding and eternal weight of glory" (2 Corinthians 4:17). While the affliction Paul mentions includes physical infirmities, it can include persecution. He informs us our afflictions are at work in us and will result in glory for eternity. Afflictions accomplish the work of a more robust faith and a life that better resembles Jesus.

Paul also sheds light on the significant time difference between persecution and glory. The former, Paul notes, lasts "but for a moment" while the latter extends for all eternity. This truth provides encouragement to everyone who ever suffered persecution. Suffering is finite, a twinkle in the continuum of time; in contrast, the glory God gives lasts forever. Understanding that truth makes persecution more bearable and persevering easier. It prompted Paul to proclaim, "For I consider that the sufferings of this present time are not worthy to be compared with the glory which shall be revealed in us" (Romans 8:18). Future glory trumps present pain. What an encouraging promise.

Paul informs us how we can take these truths and apply them, so we suffer persecution with joy and steadfastness. He says, "While we do not look at the things which are seen, but at the things which are not seen. For the things which are seen are temporary, but the things which are not seen are eternal" (2 Corinthians 4:18). When we adopt a focus on the things that are eternal, we acquire a perspective that better handles the trials and tribulations of this world. We look to the promise of His future coming, and the treasures we have stored in heaven. Consequently, the short-term pain and difficulties we experience on Earth are borne more easily. We see persecution in terms of fruit yielded for eternity, both in the growth of our faith and how it magnifies the Lord. We discussed previously how focusing on the eternal makes it easier to finish the path before us, and now learn that such focus also makes persecution and trials more bearable.

Persecution also equips us to better relate to and comfort those who similarly suffer. Paul said that just as God "comforts us in all our tribulation" we are also "able to comfort those who are in any trouble, with the comfort with which we ourselves are comforted by God" (2 Corinthians 1:4). Just as those who lose a child to death can relate to, understand, and comfort others going through such tragedy, those who suffer persecution can comfort their fellow sufferers. They can build them up in the faith and encourage them. They are able to share the positive outcome that persecution produces, such as a stronger faith, increased hope, and greater joy. Also, sharing the experience of persecution tightens the bond between believers, especially those separated by geography and governments.

One reason most of us express little interest in, or even awareness of, the tremendous persecution suffered by believers overseas is that we experience little persecution here. We cannot relate to their sufferings. We cannot appreciate their boldness in professing Christ at the risk of losing their jobs, freedom, safety, or lives. We fail to understand the depth of their faithfulness in sharing the gospel with neighbors, peers, work colleagues, and strangers despite the likelihood they will eventually land in jail or suffer harm.

Because we cannot relate, we rarely pray for them. We fail to bring them before the Lord and ask His protection on them. We do not intercede on their behalf and ask God to bless their boldness with considerable fruit. We decline to seek His blessing on them for their commitment, nor request He strengthen them to persevere. We offer no such prayers because we have yet to suffer persecution ourselves and therefore fail to understand their tremendous need for prayer. The needs of the persecuted church remain oblivious to us at the moment but we will appreciate them and their sacrifice much more once persecution increases here. As we begin to suffer real and significant persecution, we will connect with our fellow sufferers in a meaningful way and begin to pray for them with more regularity and passion. We will appreciate the comments from the writer of Hebrews who had this to say about the church that stood steadfast with him during his suffering and persecution: "You endured a great struggle with sufferings: partly while you were made a spectacle both by reproaches and tribulations, and partly while you became companions of those who were so treated; for you had compassion on me in my chains, and joyfully accepted the plundering of your goods, knowing that you have a better and an enduring possession for yourselves in heaven" (Hebrews 10:32b-34).

American Christians believe we have avoided persecution because God chose instead to bless us. We believe this blessing flows from the establishment of this country on Christian principles and the existence of a robust and vibrant church for several centuries. However true that may have been in the past, it no longer remains the case. Our culture has begun a moral nosedive that the church only mildly resists on limited fronts; in other areas the church has linked arms with society. Consequently, whatever protection from persecution God may have provided in the past, we should recognize we no longer deserve it today. We need persecution to develop the Christian attributes that tribulation yields. While none of us want to see our brethren suffer, we recognize the benefits that persecution produces. In some ways, persecution can accomplish quickly the revival and cleansing needed in the American church, which no other path will accomplish as fast or as effectively.

━━━━━━━━━━━━━━━━━━━━ QUESTIONS: ━━━━━━━━━━━━━━━━━━━━

1. How familiar are you with the global persecuted church? How often do you pray for their perseverance and fruitfulness? What prevents you from making that a priority in your prayer life?

2. How does God use persecution to mature the faith of a believer?

3. What benefits would the American church accrue if it suffered more severe persecution?

Blessed are those who are persecuted for righteousness sake, for theirs is the kingdom of heaven. Blessed are you when they revile and persecute you, and say all kinds of evil against you falsely for My sake. Rejoice and be exceedingly glad, for great is your reward in heaven, for so they persecuted the prophets who were before you.

—Matthew 5:10-12

CHAPTER 27

Responding to Persecution

We have learned that those who desire to live godly in the Lord will suffer some form of persecution. Moreover, we have gained an understanding of why God allows persecution to occur and the impact it can have on believers, individually and as a church body.

Let's turn our attention to the biblical response to persecution. From the world's perspective, those who suffer unjustly for their faith should fight back, both physically and legally. Our culture expects those subject to religious persecution to become angry at both the society persecuting them and the god who allows it. Scripture, on the other hand, outlines a very different expectation for believers subject to the trials of persecution. God's Word addresses our response to those who commit persecution, as well as our response to God for permitting it.

First, Jesus says those who suffer persecution are blessed. That perspective runs counter to what the world teaches. The world believes anyone who suffers for his faith is a fool and/or abandoned by the god he serves. Some argue that God does not love those who suffer persecution since He does not prevent it. But Jesus offers a decidedly different view. Instead of reflecting abandonment by God, such suffering demonstrates His blessing. God is pleased with those who suffer hurt, humiliation, torture, teasing, torment, and even death in His name.

In what way are we blessed? Jesus explains we receive rewards in heaven for our suffering, and we enjoy those blessings for all eternity. What an awesome promise. Our Father assures us our faithfulness in the face of persecution yields His eternal blessing and reward. That ought to excite every Christian who has suffered any form of persecution. Moreover, it should encourage us to remain faithful and steadfast in our faith when the world attacks us for our commitment to Jesus.

Additionally, Jesus tells us we should rejoice when we suffer persecution for our faith. We should be exceedingly glad we have the opportunity to suffer for our belief in Him. The joy derives from how God will use persecution to grow our faith and draw us closer to Him.

Jesus' counsel is neither conceptual nor academic. His guidance does not represent some theoretical pontification on persecution. He does not impose on His disciples and followers a burden He Himself will not bear. He practices what He preaches and His suffering establishes an example we can observe and follow. He becomes an authority on persecution a few years after His sermon when He is falsely accused by those who hate Him, tortured to the brink of death by Roman soldiers who verbally humiliate and mock Him, and eventually subjected to death on the cross.

He knows He will suffer, and He knows the pain and discouragement such suffering causes. In fact, even He asks the Father to allow the cup of persecution and death to pass from Him, if salvation for man can occur any other way (Luke 22:42). Jesus develops expertise on both suffering and on remaining steadfast in the faith when subject to persecution. We can take heart that our Lord already suffered extreme persecution and relates to our persecution when it occurs. He comforts and sustains us in the midst of suffering because He has been there and understands. His example offers a source of encouragement; we are not alone. The writer of Hebrews says, "For consider Him who endured such hostility from sinners against Himself, lest you become weary and discouraged in your souls" (Hebrews 12:3).

After Jesus' resurrection, the apostles practiced this mindset when physically beaten and verbally berated by the high priest and council of elders. After suffering that persecution, Luke tells us, "So they departed from the presence of the council, rejoicing that they were counted worthy to suffer shame for His name" (Acts 5:41). After observing Jesus' faithfulness during His suffering, the apostles adopted His perspective in response to persecution. They rejoiced over the opportunity to suffer for His name. They recognized that suffering yields eternal blessings. Interestingly, the apostles viewed suffering for Jesus as a badge of honor. Luke says they rejoiced because "they were counted worthy" to suffer for Him. Whereas culture views suffering for faith as a sign of rejection and abandonment from God, the apostles viewed it as a reflection of His blessing.

While we should not seek or provoke persecution on ourselves, we should certainly share the apostolic view and praise God if He counts us worthy to suffer tribulation. Our suffering indicates He views our faith sufficient and steadfast to withstand the world's torment and shame. Sadly, we often avoid persecution at all costs because we view it from a temporal perspective. It causes pain and discomfort to our physical bodies, results in emotional agony, and disrupts our lives. When viewed from the eternal perspective that Jesus held, believers embrace persecution as a natural and expected outcome of living boldly for the Lord.

James offers a similar perspective. He tells us, "My brethren, count it all joy when you fall into various trials, knowing that the testing of your faith produces patience" (James 1:2-3). While trials are not exclusively persecution, it certainly includes such tribulation. James echoes the earlier encouragement that we have a spirit of joy regarding trials. Why? They produce patience. Having patience matures our faith and teaches us to trust God and His timing.

Peter summarizes the above lessons really well. "Beloved, do not think it strange concerning the fiery trial which is to try you, as though some strange thing happened to you; but rejoice to the extent that you partake of Christ's suffering, that when His glory is revealed, you may also be glad with exceeding joy. If you are reproached for the name of Christ, blessed are you, for the Spirit of glory and of God rests upon you. On their part He is blasphemed, but on your part He is glorified. But let none of you suffer as a murderer, a thief, an evildoer, or as a busybody in other people's matters. Yet, if anyone suffers as a Christian, let him not be ashamed, but let him glorify God in this matter" (1 Peter 4:12-16). Let's review the salient points Peter captures in this passage.

First, the presence of persecution in our lives should not surprise us. Do not think suffering represents some unlikely or unusual burden. It occurs in the life of every Christian and occurs whenever we seek to follow and glorify Jesus.

Second, rejoicing represents the biblical response to suffering and persecution. Our Lord suffered as our example and we rejoice that He allows us to share in that experience. Moreover, by sharing Christ's suffering in this world we will share in His glory in the world to come. What a fantastic tradeoff.

Third, Peter reminds us that bearing the reproach and hate of the world reveals the presence of God and the Holy Spirit upon us. That presence demonstrates an authentic faith and reflects spiritual growth and maturation. Our suffering confirms our faith.

Fourth, Peter confirms that the blessings produced by suffering only apply when a result of our faith in Jesus and pursuit of His glory. If due to our sin, then no such blessing exists.

Fifth, glorify God whenever you suffer for your faith. Sing praise to Him that He counts you worthy to suffer on His behalf. Do not feel shame but honor for the persecution heaped on you.

QUESTIONS:

1. How should we respond to persecution? Is it difficult to praise God and rejoice when persecuted?

2. Why does the world persecute believers?

3. Can anything make suffering persecution more bearable?

PART VII

Difficult because: Deception Exists

We are almost finished. We need to examine three final ways in which the path that leads to life is difficult. Each involves the challenge of identifying truth in a sin-filled world. On the one hand, this really is not such a difficult task. Scripture is the sole source of truth and reliable on all matters of faith. We can embrace with confidence everything it says regarding God, His will, our sinfulness, the path to salvation, and His expectations for us. It reveals the person of Jesus Christ and emphasizes the importance of knowing Him personally. Understanding and living God's truth is as easy as reading and applying His Word.

The difficult part in all this is that the world wants to deceive you. The god of this age wants desperately to lead you astray. He will do everything in his power to convince you that the God of the Bible does not exist and the Bible itself is not trustworthy. Instead, he will persuade you to adopt the wisdom of the world; only then will you fully understand your purpose here and God's plan for you. Satan is especially effective at deceiving people. He understands the weakness of each person and attacks it. He cajoles, persuades, deludes, tempts, and lies in order to get someone to follow his path instead of the Lord's. Rejecting his arguments and deception requires we remain steadfast in the Word and not allow any opportunity for his schemes to take root. We must reject the wisdom of man, no matter how nicely packaged it comes.

An additional source of difficulty is that the evil one uses false teachers and pastors to provide unbiblical instruction regarding the Word of God. Increasing in number across the United States, these Christian leaders command respect because of their educational pedigree and established presence in evangelical churches and institutions. They are not easily identified; often they teach and preach lessons that contain biblical concepts and truths. But they wander from the truth in critical ways which lead listeners astray if they embrace those teachings. The fact that Christian leaders are the source of the deceptive message makes it difficult for many to resist and reject them.

With this deception playing out across the secular and religious backdrop of America, it is critical that every believer study and understand Scripture himself. Yes, we need to attend church and hear God's Word conveyed through our pastors. But we need to confirm what he says aligns with what the Bible teaches. We cannot get lazy and simply trust that he will share the truth.

We will spend the three remaining chapters exploring what God's Word says about these topics. First, we learn what Scripture teaches about the deception of our hearts. Second, we examine the wisdom of the world and how it conflicts with God's wisdom. Finally, we study what the Bible says about false prophets and how they have infested the church with their false doctrine.

The heart is deceitful above all things, and
desperately wicked; who can know it?

—Jeremiah 17:9

CHAPTER 28

Why We Misunderstand

T he truths we have explored to this point do not digest easily. They are bitter pills to swallow. We do not easily embrace these truths because they require significant change in our lives, change we resist since it makes our lives less comfortable and less pleasurable. These truths require we do difficult things that do not come naturally, such as denying self and forgiving others. Our sin nature fights these truths relentlessly. So how do we properly understand and apply these truths?

We need an accurate understanding of our heart's condition and how it wars against truth. Moreover, we need insight that reveals our heart's deceit. Finally, we must learn how to understand God's Word and fully follow it. The prophet Jeremiah provides helpful insight into the condition of our hearts. He observed, "The heart is deceitful above all things, and desperately wicked; who can know it?" (Jeremiah 17:9). We learn two valuable lessons from this verse.

First, our heart evidences deceit more than anything else. In fact, its preeminent attribute is deceit. Desperate wickedness represents its second characteristic, which drives the deceitful nature rooted in the heart. This truth runs counter to what the world believes and teaches: that man is essentially good and his nature generally honest. God's word refutes this perspective, revealing the truth that we are innately wicked. We gravitate towards evil. Our iniquity is not a garden variety; it is desperate wickedness.

Many of us cringe when told we are wicked because we view ourselves in high regard. We tend to agree with the world that we are primarily good and our hearts tend toward righteousness. We have bought into the world's view that only the most heinous crimes reflect wickedness and that everything else represents a small sin, if any sin at all. Further, we tend to agree with the world's perspective regarding the acceptability of looking out for ourselves, pursuing our own interests, and living the good life. It views such behavior favorably, as rugged independence, not steeped in selfishness. We buy into these lies because our hearts want to believe it, and they are fueled by our sin nature. We must allow God's Word to discern between what is good and holy, and what is wicked and evil. Recognizing our heart's deceitful nature is critical to rejecting the lies of society.

Second, the verse teaches that no one understands the heart. Because it operates from a position of deceit, we continually fail to understand its true condition. No man understands his own heart. Consequently, we should never base our faith on what feels right or what our heart tells us. We must rely solely on Scripture for truth. When we decide our beliefs based on what seems right to us, we fall prey to our heart's deceit. We must reject the views of culture and academia on matters of morality, truth, good, and evil. Deceit consumes worldly views because they are predicated on self. Culture celebrates self and believes our purpose lies in pursuing satisfaction and gratification. Since our hearts and the world both operate from a position of deceit and selfishness, we cannot trust either as a source for understanding truth.

Paul explains the outcome for anyone who allows his deceitful heart to dictate his faith and beliefs. "For the time will come when they will not endure sound doctrine, but according to their own desires, because they have itching ears, they will heap up for themselves teachers; and they will turn their ears away from the truth, and be turned aside to fables" (2 Timothy 4:3-4). The deceitful heart leads to the adoption of false doctrine. Since truth does not motivate it, the heart does not pursue sound doctrine. Instead it pursues a faith that allows it to achieve its own desires. The heart seeks teaching that reinforces the lifestyle it loves and imposes no burden.

God's Word makes clear that the lust of the flesh must die but the heart does not tolerate such truth. So what does it do? It seeks out pastors who teach beliefs that comport with what the heart desires. When a pastor speaks truth and makes an individual uncomfortable in his lifestyle and conduct, the heart tries to persuade him to find another church. The heart wants affirmation that its desires, actions, and pursuits of the world are acceptable.

Anyone who allows his heart to determine truth resists Scripture. He will not embrace fully what Jesus taught. Instead, he seeks and adheres to false doctrine. If your heart has resisted biblical truths covered in prior chapters, you now know why. The heart wants nothing to do with God's Word. The author of Hebrews warns us, "Beware, brethren, lest there be in any of you an evil heart of unbelief in departing from the living God" (Hebrews 3:12). Do not trust your heart to determine truth. It will lead you away from Jesus.

To whom do we turn then for truth? Hebrews informs us: "For the word of God is living and powerful, and sharper than any two-edged sword, piercing even to the division of soul and spirit, and of joints and marrow, and is a discerner of the thoughts and intents of the heart" (Hebrews 4:12). Scripture reveals itself as the source of truth. But the Bible reveals more than God's truth, it can discern our thoughts and even knows the intents of our heart. No heart can deceive God or His Word. Scripture guides us to the Lord and reveals His holiness but also exposes the deceit and wickedness of our own heart. Rather than relying on our own understanding, we need to rely on Scripture. Moreover, we need to defer to God's Word as the interpreter of truth rather than ourselves. As our hearts are wicked and deceitful, we cannot trust them to honestly interpret truth. God's Word is alive, possesses power, and will pierce the depths of our soul with its insight.

=========================== QUESTIONS: ===========================

1. What risk do you run if you allow your heart to determine what you believe?

2. How reliable is Scripture in communicating the will and mind of God?

3. Have you identified any of your beliefs as inconsistent with Scripture? What action(s) will you pursue to resolve this contradiction?

Preach the gospel, not with wisdom of words, lest the cross of Christ should be made of no effect. For the message of the cross is foolishness to those who are perishing, but to us who are being saved it is the power of God. For it is written, "I will destroy the wisdom of the wise, and bring to nothing the understanding of the prudent." Where is the wise? Where is the scribe? Where is the disputer of this age? Has not God made foolish the wisdom of this world? For since, in the wisdom of God, the world through wisdom did not know God, it pleased God through the foolishness of the message preached to save those who believe. For Jews request a sign, and the Greeks seek after wisdom; but we preach Christ crucified, to the Jews a stumbling block and to the Greeks foolishness, but to those who are called, both Jews and Greeks, Christ the power of God and the wisdom of God. Because the foolishness of God is wiser than men, and the weakness of God is stronger than men.

—1 Corinthians 1:17-25

CHAPTER 29

Avoid the World's Wisdom

The wisdom of the world attracts the rebellious heart. Worldly wisdom appeals to those who deny anything bigger than themselves, who refuse to consider a Creator because they must then address how to respond to that God. The first two chapters of 1 Corinthians discuss the wisdom of the world and contrast it with the wisdom of God. Let's explore the relevant verses to understand God's view and why we need to avoid adopting the world's wisdom.

Paul says that Christ sent him to "preach the gospel, not with wisdom of words, lest the cross of Christ should be made of no effect" (1 Corinthians 1:17), later adding that his preaching was "not with persuasive words of human wisdom, but in demonstration of the Spirit and of power" (1 Corinthians 2:4). Why did Paul avoid preaching and persuading people with human wisdom and words? Because he knew God's wisdom and man's wisdom oppose each other, and are entirely incompatible with one another. You cannot exercise the world's wisdom and understand the heart of God. Consequently, had Paul preached with the wisdom of men, he would not have preached truth with the power of the Holy Spirit.

If God's wisdom reveals truth then why do so many of us prefer the wisdom of man; why do we resist the wisdom of God? Paul addresses this question when he states that "the message of the cross is foolishness to those who are perishing" (1 Corinthians 1:18). Those who follow the wisdom of the world have pride in their heart. They think they possess the power within themselves to understand truth, and therefore do not need God to reveal it to them. Their pride constructs the view that only intellectually advanced individuals can understand truth.

God hates the pride and inflated egos exhibited by those who believe they can understand Him on their own terms and exercising their own wisdom. So God chose the foolishness of the cross to reveal His Son and provide salvation, because the proud find such a path appalling. Those wise in their own eyes, who believe their intelligence leads them to truth, invariably reject the foolish path to salvation. God refuses to allow man to determine his own route to eternal life, "For the wisdom of this world is foolishness with God" (1 Corinthians 3:19).

Instead, God looks for the broken in spirit who recognize that absent His intercession they cannot know truth. He rejects the wisdom of the world because "the world through wisdom did not know God" therefore "it pleased God through the foolishness of the message preached to save those who believe" (1 Corinthians 1:21). God knows the world views with derision the call of Christ and the message of the cross. They deem such beliefs utter foolishness. He revels in the fact that an arrogant and self-consumed world rejects His wisdom. Their response aligns with His design. Paul observed that the message of Christ crucified would represent a stumbling block for the Jews and to the gentiles foolishness (1 Corinthians 1:23). Those who follow the world's wisdom always reject God because the proud heart can have it no other way. Therefore, "God has chosen the foolish things of the world to put to shame the wise" (1 Corinthians 1:27).

Any attempt to make the gospel logical to the world inevitably perverts it, so the gospel loses its power. Paul states he preached so the faith of converts would "not be in the wisdom of men but in the power of God" (1 Corinthians 2:5). Because America celebrates and emphasizes human wisdom, too many believers attempt to make the cross of Christ more intellectually palatable for others. We must avoid doing so. We must resist the urge to soften the foolish nature of the cross, for that is where the power exists.

Those who intellectualize the message of the cross err in their understanding of how God calls people to Him. They incorrectly assume that what prevents people from embracing Jesus is the content of the message. If only the church preached a less demanding gospel, they exclaim, it would appeal to a far wider audience. Sand down the rough edges, ignore those components that run counter to our modern culture, and mitigate any obligation on the part of potential believers, and the gospel will thrive. What thrives, though, is an apostate gospel that brings people no closer to Jesus than when they were unaware of Him. Those who accept such teaching are done an incredible disservice; they are sold a gospel that does not bring salvation. What results is the proliferation of believers in intellect only, who are not believers at all.

What we fail to realize is that God calls whom He calls. He has already revealed Himself to all mankind so "His invisible attributes are clearly seen, being understood by the things that are made, even His eternal power and Godhead, so that they are without excuse" (Romans 1:20). Within all people lies an innate awareness for the one true God. Whether one pursues the object of that awareness and seeks a relationship with Him rests with each individual. Most reject the opportunity to learn about God choosing instead to create a god who can serve them, rather than serving the Lord. They view themselves too smart to accept God as revealed. Consequently, they become fools in the eyes of God (Romans 1:22). Their self-professed wisdom leads to futile thoughts and foolish hearts which darken to the things of God, so much that they actually "changed the glory of the incorruptible God into an image made like corruptible man" and "who exchanged the truth of God for the lie, and worshiped and served the creature rather than the Creator" (Romans 1:23, 25).

So where does the wisdom of the world lead? It rejects the Creator God and embraces as god that which He created. Where does worldly wisdom exist? In the hearts of those whose rebellion has blinded them from God and His truth; it appeals to those who celebrate themselves as the god of their destinies. They reject God and instead deify the world and the things of the world. Such belief represents the arrogance of the flesh.

Is it any wonder God hates the wisdom of the world, that He chooses the foolish things to put to shame the wise? No surprise then that Paul avoided the wisdom of words to convince the gentiles. He says the wisdom of the world is foolishness to God, and the wisdom of Christ is foolishness to the world. God's truth requires we recognize our own shortcomings, sin, and smallness; in contrast, the flesh exalts and glorifies itself as master of its own fate.

Matthew tells us Jesus condemned those cities where He did much of His work, since they refused to repent (see Matthew 11:20). Jesus informed them that immense judgment would result from their unbelief. It is remarkable that thousands of people observed Jesus in person and yet rejected His truth and teachings. How could so many people experience the presence of the living God and ignore their need for repentance? Jesus explains: "I thank you, Father, Lord of heaven and earth, because You have hidden these things from the wise and prudent and have revealed them to babes" (Matthew 11:25). Jesus communicates a powerful insight we need to understand and apply. God's truth does not come from education or common sense; it comes from His revelation alone. No amount of study, no theology degree, no spiritual experience yields His wisdom. His Spirit reveals it as He wills. The Bible provides examples of God revealing His truth to those who seek Him, despite their absence of formal training or an advanced degree.

In Acts 4, we observe Peter and John arrested for preaching the gospel of Christ. They are brought before the Jewish leaders and the high priest to respond to the charges and give an account of what they have done. Peter gives a brief overview of the gospel, pointing out that Jesus alone is the author of salvation. We are told he preached with boldness. This surprised the leaders and observers because both John and Peter were "uneducated and untrained men" (Acts 4:13). Their ability to preach the gospel in clear, compelling, and bold terms was not consistent with what one would expect from an unlearned or untrained individual. As a result, Scripture tells us those present "marveled" at Peter and John.

That succinctly captures the view of the world. Absent education and formal training, no one expects to perform well at his craft or advance far within his career. The world sees from experience those who are trained to lay bricks become much better bricklayers than those untrained. Similarly, those educated to become physicists better understand the miracles of the universe and how it functions than those uneducated. So the world (and often the church) applies the same principle to matters of faith. Who better to offer insight into the Word of God than an educated pastor who has studied at a university? Who better to speak on what Scripture means in today's culture than one trained at a seminary? But that perspective runs counter to what Scripture tell us. Scripture never implies that formal education and training yield an understanding of truth.

Curiously, some Christian leaders believe they best understand God's Word because of their training. They are blind to what the Bible teaches as to who understands Scripture and gains spiritual insight. If they misunderstand and fail to accurately communicate truth on this subject, what qualifies them to teach truth on other matters? It is a sober reminder that we must exercise considerable caution before trusting what we hear from Christian leaders and pastors.

So if education and training do not yield insight into God's Word, what does? The passage from Acts 4 reveals two things necessary to understand God's truth and preach it with power. First, Luke informs us Peter was "filled with the Holy Spirit" (Acts 4:8) as he began to talk to the Jewish leaders and the crowd. It is the Holy Spirit who gives us supernatural wisdom. He reveals truth and provides us the words to preach. Jesus made the same point when He noted that we need not fear what to say at times of persecution, for the Holy Spirit will speak through us (Mark 13:11). Absent the Holy Spirit, no one speaks the truth of God's word nor understands the mysteries of Scripture. They are God's and He chooses to reveal them to whom He chooses through His Spirit. No amount of formal training or studying at elite universities reveals these truths and insights. They are not the worlds', so the tools of the world can never explain them.

A second factor equipped Peter and John with the wisdom and power to preach truth. Luke tells us the crowd "realized that they had been with Jesus" (Acts 4:13). Those who want the power of God in their preaching need to draw close and develop a deeper, more intimate relationship with Him. Pray more frequently, seek His will more diligently, and embed His word in your heart more faithfully. As you do, you will understand more clearly His truth and share your faith with power.

Thousands of evangelical churches exist across the United States, most of which declare a biblically sound doctrinal statement. Why then so little power in the American church today? Why does the church have so little boldness against the culture? Why does our society sink into greater spiritual darkness, becoming increasingly wicked and evil? Why does the church resist so little and shed so little light on the culture? According to God's word, the absence of Jesus in our lives and the absence of the Holy Spirit in our preaching accounts for it.

While none of us can judge the heart of another, we can observe the lack of impact the church has on society and understand the condition of its collective heart. One conclusion explains the disparity between what we profess to believe as evangelicals and our slight impact in harvesting souls and turning this country upside down for God: we have been with Jesus too little. As a result, the Holy Spirit is not at work in many of our lives. Among believers in this nation, if each of us invested significant time alone with Jesus, in prayer, studying His Word, and listening for His guidance, we would have the same impact on the United States as the apostles had on Asia Minor.

Our inability to impact culture is not due to its wickedness, rebellion, and antipathy to God. Rather, our casual relationship with Jesus results in our nation becoming increasingly wicked, rebellious, and hateful to God. As with the church of Ephesus, we have left our first love (Revelation 2:4). While we believe the right things and say the right prayers, too often we have no deep, abiding love for Jesus and spend too little time with Him. And our country suffers as a result.

As we conclude let's examine a passage from Isaiah 14. He describes a man who takes a tree and with half of it starts a fire and roasts a meal, thus satisfying his hunger. The other half he "makes into a god. His carved image. He falls down before it and worships it, prays to it and says, 'deliver me, for you are my god'" (Isaiah 44:17). Now it seems insane that someone would create an idol with his own hands and then show it reverence and praise as though it were a god. How could anyone believe the work of the craftsman is his god? Isaiah explains such actions are done by those who "do not know nor understand; for He has shut their eyes so that they cannot see, and their hearts so that they cannot understand" (Isaiah 44:18). God closes eyes and hearts from understanding the truth and recognizing sin, because of the hardness of hearts. He keeps such people in darkness and withholds wisdom and understanding from them.

Paul speaks similarly when discussing the coming of the lawless one at the end times. In view of how much Scripture addresses the antichrist, how can those alive at that time fail to identify him? They fall to his deception and perish "because they did not receive the love of the truth, that they might be saved" (2 Thessalonians 2:10). In other words, because they rejected the truth of Jesus and decline His offer of grace and mercy, God has given them up to deception and "will send them strong delusion that they should believe the lie" (2 Thessalonians 2:11).

What application do these two lessons have on our lives: Isaiah twenty-five hundred years ago and the coming antichrist in the near future? In both instances, people embrace a spiritual path that leads to destruction and eternal death. They reject truth that God presents them. As a result, God gives them over to false beliefs and blinds them to Him. Since they do not genuinely desire to know the one true God, He permits their delusion.

We ought to understand the broader lesson here. God offers His truth and mercy to all who genuinely seek Him. Those who diligently desire to know His truth will find it, and find Him. In contrast, He deludes those who pursue their own truth and create their own view of god. I fear many of us have embraced part of the gospel but do not desire God's call on our entire lives. Many of us express little interest in knowing truth unless it aligns with our preconceived view of truth. As a result, we run the danger of falling into the same trap as the craftsmen Isaiah observed and those alive at the end days: God darkens our understanding and allows us to believe the lie we desire. If we pursue the wisdom of this world, that path awaits us. On the other hand, we can pursue the wisdom of the Lord and embrace His truth. The world will label us fools, but we will have the confidence of eternal life through the presence of the Holy Spirit. And that makes each of us a very special fool.

1. What does the wisdom of the world represent? Why does God hate it?

2. What does the wisdom of God represent? Why does the world hate it?

3. What risk exists for anyone choosing to apply the wisdom of the world in defining his faith?

Beware of false prophets who come to you in sheep's clothing, but inwardly they are ravenous wolves.

—Matthew 7:15

CHAPTER 30

Beware False Teachers

J esus warns of false prophets and how they operate. They are not obvious. They do not look demonic or spew offensive and ridiculous doctrine. They appear respectable, are engaging, and connect easily with others. They teach doctrine society finds palatable and our culture deems acceptable. Most false prophets reference Scripture in their teaching, giving the impression of biblical soundness. They present unsound doctrine so cleverly it sounds correct. Therefore, we must exercise diligence in studying Scripture so we do not succumb to their deceit, for it leads to death.

Paul explains, "For I know this, that after my departure savage wolves will come in among you, not sparing the flock. Also from among yourselves men will rise up, speaking perverse things, to draw away the disciples after themselves" (Acts 20:29-30). False leaders come from within the church and establish themselves as leaders among the faithful. Identifying them is difficult because they project credibility and acceptance in the Christian community. However, irrespective of how respectable a teacher's credentials, how godly he appears, or how much good he accomplishes, we must confirm he preaches the Word without deceit. If at any time he begins to teach a gospel contrary to Scripture, he must be rebuked.

Peter explains more about these false teachers. "But there were also false prophets among the people, even as there will be false teachers among you, who will secretly bring in destructive heresies, even denying the Lord who bought them, and bring on themselves swift destruction. And many will follow their destructive ways, because of whom the way of truth will be blasphemed" (2 Peter 2:1-2). Peter stresses that false teachers are at work among us; in our seminaries, churches and Bible study groups. They have infiltrated the ranks of authors and recording artists sold at the local Christian book store. Many are pastors, counselors and reputable Christian leaders. We do not easily identify them because they teach heresy secretively. They intertwine references to Scripture with their commentary that sounds appealing. That combination attracts many believers who eventually follow these false teachers. Peter observes that the teaching leads to destruction, for the instructor and the follower, highlighting the importance of identifying and rejecting false teaching.

Peter later identifies a key attribute of false prophets. He informs us "They have a heart trained in covetous practices" (2 Peter 2:14). They embrace a spirit of covetousness and the god of this age has trained them to preach doctrine steeped in covetous practices. The heresy they teach has a foundation in covetousness. Since many of us in the American church struggle with covetousness, we easily fall prey to such teaching. In fact, Peter identifies that sin as the reason so many embrace heresy, declaring, "By covetousness they will exploit you with deceptive words" (2 Peter 2:3).

False prophets conduct themselves with deception but employ covetousness to facilitate that deception. Those exploited with deceit remain culpable since their susceptibility to deception results from the covetous spirit they harbor. They covet a message that appeals to the flesh and legitimizes their covetous lifestyles. In addition to the previous dangers identified with a covetous lifestyle, we also learn it makes us vulnerable to the exploits of false teachers. Covetousness does more than decay our faith, create a barrier to God, and operate as a form of idolatry. It facilitates our willingness to embrace deceitful doctrine. It blinds us to truth.

Peter builds on this theme, adding, "For when they speak great swelling words of emptiness, they allure, through the lusts of the flesh, through licentiousness, the ones who have actually escaped from those who live in error" (2 Peter 2:18). The words spoken by false teachers have no substance in truth. Void of the Holy Spirit, they sound impressive but yield no good thing. They do, however, allure those in the church. Peter explains we are magnetized by false teaching through the lusts of our flesh. Our covetous nature predisposes us to accept insights offered by false prophets. God's Word makes no such appeal to our flesh. Our covetousness surrenders to the empty words of deceit.

In fact, our receptivity to false teaching actually leads us to seek teachers who train in lies and deceit. We desire instruction that affirms our worldly decisions and behavior. Paul told Timothy, "For the time will come when they will not endure sound doctrine, but according to their own desires, because they have itching ears, they will heap up for themselves teachers; and they will turn their ears away from the truth and be turned aside to fables" (2 Timothy 4:3-4).

These verses crystallize the driving force behind false doctrine and apostasy in America. Our sin-nature demands we follow doctrine appealing to self. Un-crucified, our flesh flourishes and dictates our decisions, even exercising influence over what we believe. Instead of the Spirit guiding us in truth and matters of faith, we defer to our flesh. As a result, we seek truth that pleases us and embrace teaching that affirms us. Whereas the Spirit challenges us and leads us to reject our interests, the flesh celebrates them. The two doctrines are incompatible. We must resist any doctrine our flesh finds palatable and which demands nothing from us.

One false doctrine many pursue involves balancing faith in Jesus with adherence to the world's philosophy. It seeks to blend the two beliefs, though a merger always requires compromising faith. Paul emphasizes the direct correlation between pursuing the world's wisdom and rejecting faith. "O Timothy! Guard what was committed to your trust, avoiding the profane and vain babblings and contradictions of what is falsely called knowledge—by professing it, some have strayed concerning the faith" (1 Timothy 6:20-21). The world's wisdom does not lead to an enlightened state, as promised. It deceives and leads down a path of foolishness and folly, resulting in death. It cannot exist with true faith but always leads followers astray.

The demise of sound doctrine and increase in false teaching should surprise no one. Paul warns us. "Let no one deceive you by any means; for that Day will not come unless the falling away comes first, and the man of sin is revealed, the son of perdition" (2 Thessalonians 2:3). As the day of the Lord approaches, the church increasingly embraces deceit and false prophets. Their deception grows so severe that eventually a falling away occurs, the apostate church. The proliferation of false teaching and deceptive doctrine certainly indicates that time is nearing, perhaps even at the door.

Paul references this falling away by some believers when he writes Timothy asserting "Now the Spirit expressly says that in latter times some will depart from the faith, giving heed to deceiving spirits and doctrines of demons" (1 Timothy 4:1). Paul confirms that some will leave the faith in the end days. In fact, he notes that the Spirit affirms this. Paul then adds an interesting wrinkle regarding deceptive doctrine. He attributes the spirit world as its source. Deceiving spirits and demons disseminate deceptive doctrine through false prophets. The god of this age and his demonic army create lies and then use false prophets to broadcast those heresies.

What motivates false prophets? Paul informs Timothy they are "men of corrupt minds and destitute of the truth, who suppose that godliness is a means of gain" (1 Timothy 6:5). These men recognize that appearing godly can lead to achieving their worldly lusts. Whether wealth, status, influence, power, income, or other worldly gain, false prophets cast themselves as Christian leaders in pursuit of those temporal benefits. They possess no genuine faith in Jesus, nor desire one. The things of this world motivate them. That explains why they operate with a spirit of covetousness.

Before we close the chapter, we need to address a final question. How do we identify false doctrine and avoid false prophets? How can each believer identify and reject unbiblical teaching? Identifying apostate teaching requires diligence and guidance from the Holy Spirit, but nothing more difficult than that. Anyone who desires God's truth can recognize instruction contradicting it.

Read God's Word regularly and study Scripture. Equipped with an understanding of truth, you perceive false teaching more easily. Satan's lies influence and deceive us less as we build and maintain a foundation on the Bible. A heart imbued with God's wisdom is far less susceptible to false teaching. False teachers would encounter no receptivity in church if all believers knew the Bible well. Test what others teach. Avoid simply reading references provided since false doctrine often takes a Bible verse entirely out of context. Examine what other Scripture says. Understand the broader context of each passage. Finally, pray for guidance from the Holy Spirit.

R. Roderick Cyr

QUESTIONS:

1. What does the Bible tell us about the increase in false prophets? What does this indicate?

2. Why are so many people who profess faith in Jesus led astray by false gospels?

3. What single strategy can we employ to prevent the adoption of false doctrine in our faith?

AFTERWORD

We have explored many biblical passages that capture the guidance and commands Jesus gave His followers. Obeying many of these can be difficult because our sinful and rebellious nature resists. But Jesus never softened or obscured the truth about following Him. He consistently and explicitly emphasized the challenging nature a life of discipleship represents.

Despite the clarity and frequency with which Jesus spoke to His expectations, and the subsequent apostolic epistles that reinforce them, many of us remain convinced that God desires to bless us with lives of comfort, ease, and the riches of this world. We want to continue our worldly lifestyles and simply become religious in our words and appearance. The deceitfulness of our hearts, the world, and sometimes even Christian leaders persuade many of us that this represents a viable option. But it represents a broad path traveled by many and its way leads to destruction. So how do we avoid this path? How can we know that we genuinely believe and possess authentic faith?

Paul offers this advice: "Examine yourselves as to whether you are in the faith. Prove yourselves. Do you not know yourselves, that Jesus Christ is in you—unless indeed you are disqualified" (2 Corinthians 13:5). Take this challenge very seriously. Examine yourself. Examine your faith. Examine your heart.

1. Examine your lifestyle: does it reflect selfishness or sacrifice?
2. Examine your priorities: Do they mirror the world's or the Lord's?

3. Examine your passions: Are they for the "cares of this world" or knowing Jesus more intimately?
4. Examine your time: Do you spend it on achieving your agenda or advancing God's kingdom?
5. Examine your focus: Is it on temporal, material things or on that with eternal value?

Genuine faith always results in lives substantially changed. The work of the Holy Spirit convicts us to leave our lifestyles of sin and pursue God in each area of life. We have examined numerous Scripture that validate this truth unequivocally. If you want to know whether you have sincere belief in the Lord, examine your life. The evidence is there.

Paul issues a second challenge in this verse. Prove you possess genuine faith. Prove it in your decisions, your use of time, how you administer your income, how you treat others (your spouse, kids, neighbors, and strangers), your relationship with the Lord, and your thoughts, desires, and daily pursuits. Prove it every day. And as you do you will experience spiritual maturation. God will transform you in ways you never imagined and your life will reflect the fruit of the Spirit. Moreover, you will bear fruit for His kingdom and impact for eternity those around you. Remember Jesus' words: "He who abides in Me, and I in him, bears much fruit" (John 15:5). Are you bearing fruit? What evidence do you have in response to Paul's challenge to prove your faith?

In closing, I want to remind you that God loves you very much. He wants a healthy, growing relationship with you. We should not confuse His deep love, though, with a desire to please us and make us happy. He wants us to align our lives to His will and become more like Jesus in every way. As our example, Jesus did not live a life of ease, comfort, and self-fulfillment. Instead, He lived wholly obedient to His Father. That resulted in a difficult life, including betrayal by one of His apostles, denial by others, false allegations, ridicule, and a brutal death on the cross. Our obedience will lead to difficulties as well. That should surprise none of us now that we know Jesus told of the challenges ahead, declaring: "difficult is the path that leads to life." Sadly, the life of difficulty Jesus offers anyone who follows Him attracts few of us in America where we tend to avoid difficult lives. In a culture where advertising promotes ease, idolizes self, celebrates luxury and promises happiness, a marketer could not have created a less appealing slogan than "Follow Jesus, His way is difficult." Yet that represents the opportunity He provides us. It is not a life for the fainthearted.

CPSIA information can be obtained at www.ICGtesting.com
Printed in the USA
BVOW041955160413

318339BV00009B/337/P